Felix Heidenreich, Florian Weber-Stein
The Politics of Digital Pharmacology

Political Science | Volume 135

This open access publication was enabled by the support of POLLUX – Informationsdienst Politikwissenschaft

and a network of academic libraries for the promotion of the open-access-transformation in the Social Sciences and Humanities (transcript Open Library Community Politik 2022).

Vollsponsoren: Freie Universität Berlin – Universitätsbibliothek | Staatsbibliothek zu Berlin | Universitätsbibliothek der Humboldt-Universität zu Berlin | Universitätsbibliothek Bielefeld | Universitätsbibliothek der Ruhr-Universität Bochum | Universitäts- und Landesbibliothek Bonn | Staats- und Universitätsbibliothek Bremen | Universitäts- und Landesbibliothek Darmstadt | Sächsische Landesbibliothek Staats- und Universitätsbibliothek Dresden (SLUB) | Universitäts- und Landesbibliothek Düsseldorf | Universitätsbibliothek Frankfurt am Main | Justus-Liebig-Universität Gießen | Niedersächsische Staats- und Universitätsbibliothek Göttingen | Universitätsbibliothek der FernUniversität in Hagen | Staats- und Universitätsbibliothek Carl von Ossietzky, Hamburg | Gottfried Wilhelm Leibniz Bibliothek - Niedersächsische Landesbibliothek | Technische Informationsbibliothek (TIB Hannover) | Universitätsbibliothek Kassel | Universitätsbibliothek Kiel (CAU) | Universitätsbibliothek Koblenz · Landau | Universitäts- und Stadtbibliothek Köln | Universitätsbibliothek Leipzig | Universitätsbibliothek Marburg | Universitätsbibliothek der Ludwig-Maximilians-Universität München | Max Planck Digital Library (MPDL) | Universität der Bundeswehr München | Universitäts- und Landesbibliothek Münster | Universitätsbibliothek Erlangen-Nürnberg | Bibliotheks- und Informationssystem der Carl von Ossietzky Universität Oldenburg | Universitätsbibliothek Osnabrück | Universitätsbibliothek Passau | Universitätsbibliothek Vechta | Universitätsbibliothek Wuppertal | Vorarlberger Landesbibliothek | Universität Wien Bibliotheks- und Archivwesen | Zentral- und Hochschulbibliothek Luzern | Universitätsbibliothek St. Gallen | Zentralbibliothek Zürich

Sponsoring Light: Bundesministerium der Verteidigung | ifa (Institut für Auslandsbeziehungen), Bibliothek | Landesbibliothek Oldenburg | Ostbayerische Technische Hochschule Regensburg, Hochschulbibliothek | ZHAW Zürcher Hochschule für Angewandte Wissenschaften, Hochschulbibliothek

Mikrosponsoring: Stiftung Wissenschaft und Politik (SWP) - Deutsches Institut für Internationale Politik und Sicherheit | Leibniz-Institut für Europäische Geschichte

Felix Heidenreich is a philosopher and political scientist teaching at Universität Stuttgart. Among his publications are textbooks on political theory and contributions on Foucault and Blumenberg.

Florian Weber-Stein is a professor of political science and political education at Pädagogische Hochschule Ludwigsburg. His research interests include democratic theory and data literacy.

Felix Heidenreich, Florian Weber-Stein
The Politics of Digital Pharmacology
Exploring the Craft of Collective Care

[transcript]

The joint project "KOALA - Building and expanding cooperation in all teaching subjects" is funded by the Baden-Württemberg Ministry of Science, Research and the Arts as part of the "Teacher Training in Baden-Württemberg" funding program.

professional
school of
education
stuttgart
ludwigsburg

Bibliographic information published by the Deutsche Nationalbibliothek
The Deutsche Nationalbibliothek lists this publication in the Deutsche Nationalbibliografie; detailed bibliographic data are available in the Internet at http://dnb.d-nb.de

This work is licensed under the Creative Commons Attribution-Non Commercial 4.0 (BY-NC) license, which means that the text may be may be remixed, build upon and be distributed, provided credit is given to the author, but may not be used for commercial purposes.
For details go to: http://creativecommons.org/licenses/by-nc/4.0/
Permission to use the text for commercial purposes can be obtained by contacting rights@transcript-publishing.com
Creative Commons license terms for re-use do not apply to any content (such as graphs, figures, photos, excerpts, etc.) not original to the Open Access publication and further permission may be required from the rights holder. The obligation to research and clear permission lies solely with the party re-using the material.

First published in 2022 by transcript Verlag, Bielefeld
© Felix Heidenreich, Florian Weber-Stein

Cover layout: Maria Arndt, Bielefeld
Cover illustration: "South Bank Circle", 1991. © Richard Long. Photo: Tate
Proofread: Peter Fenn
Printed by Majuskel Medienproduktion GmbH, Wetzlar
Print-ISBN 978-3-8376-6249-8
PDF-ISBN 978-3-8394-6249-2
EPUB-ISBN 978-3-7328-6249-8
https://doi.org/10.14361/9783839462492
ISSN of series: 2702-9050
eISSN of series: 2702-9069

Printed on permanent acid-free text paper.

Contents

Foreword 7

Part I: Towards a Cura Publica

Chapter 1: Introducing Pharmacology 11
1.1　The digital onslaught: some basic considerations 11
1.2　Metaphors / analogies / comparisons:
　　　approaches to the concept of "pharmacology" 15

Chapter 2: Pharmacology on the Threshold of Modernity: Rousseau . 25
2.1　Illness as social pathology 25
2.2　Rousseau and the genesis of modern self-medication 31
2.3　Homeopathic self-medication: self-education through writing? 37
2.4　Culture as a homeopathic remedy: civic education
　　　through the theater? 41
2.5　The limits of homeopathy in Rousseau 46

Chapter 3: Digital Pharmacology: Stiegler 51
3.1　Going beyond Rousseau with Rousseau 51
3.2　Digital Grammatization I or: from the 'reading brain'
　　　to the 'twitter brain' 57
3.3　Digital Grammatization II or: friendship in the 'digital anthill' 60
3.4　Digital Grammatization III or: the alphabetization
　　　of image consciousness 63

Chapter 4: Exploring the Limits of Pharmacology 67
4.1   Homeopathic, allopathic, and heteropathic pharmacology 67
4.2   How to do political pharmacology: 'liberal' or 'republican' 70
4.3   The toolbox of digital pharmacology 72
4.4   A community of learning citizens: towards a cura publica........... 80

Part II: An Interview with Bernard Stiegler

Bernard Stiegler: Elements of Pharmacology
An interview with Felix Heidenreich and Florian Weber-Stein 85
    Concept, analogy, metaphor, art 85
    No ontology of *pharmaka*, but savoir-faire 91
    The subject of pharmacology: auto-therapy 95
    The writing self and the digital self 98
    A school of pharmacology 111

Bibliography 117
    Works by Bernard Stiegler 117
    Other cited works 118

Foreword

A few months before Bernard Stiegler came to Stuttgart in January 2020, he agreed to do an interview focusing on the concept of digital pharmacology. We finally met in the early afternoon of January 20th in the lobby of his hotel near the Public Library of Stuttgart, where his key-note lecture was to take place in the evening. We had planned to talk for about an hour at the most, to make sure that he would have the time to concentrate before the evening event. Some three hours later we were still in deep conversation. Having totally lost track of time, we suddenly needed to end our talk and hurry to the library so as not to be late for the event. Even after the public lecture, our conversation was resumed in a nearby restaurant.

Bernard Stiegler's energy and passion continued to fascinate us when we talked to him via the internet while working on the interview. In the summer of 2020, we had just sent him a transcript of our long conversation when the news of his death arrived. We were shocked. His death came completely unexpectedly, although he had told us he was suffering from a severe illness.

We are thankful that we had the chance to get to know him personally. As we continued to work on this book, his voice echoed in our minds. It is rare to meet a philosopher who is so completely dedicated to his work, so focused on intellectual endeavor and still so friendly, so welcoming and so generous. We were deeply impressed by his personal blend of seriousness and outstanding creativity, a rare combination. We hope that this book will pass on the energy we experienced in Bernard Stiegler. We would also like to thank his daughter Barbara Stiegler for allowing us to publish the interview.

This book is a result of a project funded by the *Professional School of Education (PSE)* in Stuttgart and Ludwigsburg, organized and carried out by the *International Center for Cultural and Technological Studies (IZKT)* of the University of Stuttgart together with the *University of Education in Ludwigsburg*. We would like to thank the PSE for the support.

Felix Heidenreich & Florian Weber-Stein, Stuttgart and Ludwigsburg

Part I: Towards a Cura Publica

Chapter 1: Introducing Pharmacology

1.1 The digital onslaught: some basic considerations

The influx of *digital pharmaka* into our societies poses, without any doubt, an epochal challenge. The dystopia of a digital "surveillance capitalism"[1] combined with the brutal repression of an authoritarian regime is the most horrific scenario currently being discussed in the open societies. In China it is already in place. But even if this worst-case scenario of a repressive regime can be avoided, the cultural ramifications of digitalization are unsettling. Attention-disorder has become a widespread phenomenon; mental-illness is a growing problem. It is hard to track these causalities, but it must be assumed that these effects are only the tip of the iceberg. The influx of new technologies is fundamentally transforming the way couples, families, communities interact.

We still do not really understand the profound change that modern societies are facing, this "great transformation" our culture is undergoing as these technologies are becoming ubiquitous. However, in the confrontation between different generations the level of transformation sometimes becomes evident: When "digital natives" born after 1995 and those from the elder generation (intellectually socialized with books) meet, it sometimes seems to be an encounter of two different species, different brains, different ways of Being-in-the-world.

---

1 Zuboff, Soshana: Surveillance Capitalism. The Fight for a Human Future at the New Frontier of Power, London: Profile Books 2019.

This observation does not imply a moral or aesthetic judgement; we should not object to the younger generation's brains being formatted in a different way. We should, however, take seriously the question of what the obvious technological generation gap actually means, what it implies for the present and the future, and how we can cope with this tectonic shift. "What is going on?" might be the most simple and blunt way of posing this question. The impression that in as short a time as 20 years our way of living and thinking should have changed profoundly, has not, we assume, just arisen by chance. We are witnessing a historical transformation of our mental infrastructure.

The economic, political and cultural ramifications of this transformation are not yet fully clear, although for about 30 years countless books and articles have tried to conceptualize this transformation.[2] To what degree is the enormous inequality in wealth caused by the accumulation of capital resulting from scaling-effects in the digital economy?[3] To what degree can the new populist and authoritarian movements (and regimes!) be explained by the revolution on the information market caused by the internet?[4] Is it the feeling of

---

2   Pars pro toto: Rheingold, Howard: The Virtual Community. Homesteading on the Electronic Frontier, Reading: Addison-Wesley Publishing Company 1993; Shapiro, Andrew: The Control Revolution. How the Internet Is Putting Individuals in Charge and Changing the World We Know, New York: Public Affairs, 2000; Benkler, Yochai: The Wealth of Networks. How Social Production Transforms Markets and Freedom, New Haven/London: Yale UP 2007; Castells, Manuel: The Rise of the Network Society. The Information Age: Economy, Society, and Culture. Volume I (orig. 1996), John Wiley & Sons: New York, 2nd edition, 2011.

3   Cinnamon, Jonathan: "Social Injustice in Surveillance Capitalism", in: Surveillance & Society 15 (2017), pp. 609–625.

4   Diamond, Larry: "The Road to Digital Unfreedom: The Threat of Postmodern Totalitarianism", in: Journal of Democracy 30 (2019), pp. 20–24; Harari, Yuval Noah: "Why Technology Favors Tyranny", in: The Atlantic (2018), https://www.theatlantic.com/magazine/archive/2018/10/yuval-noah-harari-technology-tyranny/568330/ (01.02.2022); Tufekci, Zeynep: "How social media took us from Tahrir Square to Donald Trump", in: MIT Technology Review

"not being heard", inevitably produced in a world in which everybody else is constantly heard — which causes some people to feel excluded? And finally: to what degree is the new wave of mental illness linked to the influx of omnipresent digital media into our "lifeworld"?

Empirical research is trying to do its best to understand these processes while they are occurring. Hegel claimed that only when night is falling will the owl of Minerva start to fly and examine the ruins of an epoch from an adequate distance: historical formations need to have ended in order to be transparent to our understanding, Hegel thought. Only when the flower is already entering the stage of decomposition, can its essence be conceptualized, he claimed. This seems to be true for the feudal society so well described by Marc Bloch[5] long after it ended. Maybe we will only have a complete, i.e. "Hegelian", picture of the digital age once it begins to morph into something new.

This Hegelian approach, however, does not seem viable in our current situation: we need to understand the storm we are caught in as fast as possible in order to survive it. And this, of course, is what the empirical study of digitalization and its effects is trying to do: to make sense of the fundamental shift in our "being-in-the-world". We can already see what digitalization can cause and will continue to induce in our societies. In order to assess these effects, it is not sufficient to list advantages and disadvantages, or to call for a "responsible" use of new technologies. It will also take a theoretical and philosophical effort to understand "what is going on". Empirical research will provide much of what is needed, but not all that is sufficient for this endeavor. In a way, Heidegger's strange dictum "the essence of technology is not technological"[6] still seems

---

(2018), https://www.technologyreview.com/2018/08/14/240325/how-social-media-took-us-from-tahrir-square-to-donald-trump/ (01.02.2022).

5   Bloch, Marc: Feudal Society, 2 Volumes, Chicago: The University of Chicago Press 1961.

6   The original phrase can be found at the beginning of his essay "The Essence of Technology" ("So ist denn auch das Wesen der Technik ganz und gar nichts Technisches".) Hannah Arendt, interestingly, had marked and com-

to point to a relevant structural problem: in order to understand a Beethoven sonata, it is not sufficient to understand how a piano is constructed or what sound frequencies are produced. The technological set-up of the digital age is just the instrument on which the music is being played. The technological dimension, that is, is not the essence of this new technology. There is something in this technology which "transcends" its technological foundations. The essence of *digital pharmaka* is thus not actually digital itself.

A theoretical or philosophical contribution to these attempts will consist, of course, first and foremost in providing conceptual tools. These conceptual tools will not only be specific terminologies, but will consist also of analogies, metaphors, and comparisons. This essay will propose and try to apply a conceptual framework which Bernard Stiegler first introduced, and then, partly also in dialogue with us, elaborated on at greater length: we feel that the term "digital pharmacology", and more generally the concept of the *pharmakon*, is extremely helpful in attempting to understand human interaction with digital media — and not only with digital media.

In Stiegler's view a skillful way of applying *pharmaka* would counterbalance a tendency towards entropy: neg-entropy, the process of 'bringing together', of gathering, convening, assembling elements is the appropriate antidote against the destructive effects of the digital onslaught. This art of fighting entropy, of working for neg-entropy finds an esthetic expression in Richard Long's work. When he creates a circle of stones as on the cover photo we have chosen for this book, an archaic technique of 'bringing together' is displayed. Working for neg-entropy seems to connect us with the most ancient practices of structuring a life-world, of bringing order into chaos.

In a rudimentary sense, this is literally an "essay": we intend to test whether the idea of digital pharmacology will help us to understand more deeply "what is going on".

---

mented on many phrases in her copy of this text, but not this decisive sentence. See: https://www.bard.edu/library/arendt/pdfs/Heidegger-TechnikundKehre.pdf.

Putting the question in such unacademic terms not only expresses a certain disorientation caused by the complexity of the subject. It also allows us to point to the entanglement of the different layers of the problem: there is something "going on" on the level of technology, of culture, of politics, and of "psycho-power" at the same time. Trying to think through the interactions between these different levels, to view them as *one thing* going on, presupposes not hiding in the corner of a well-defined academic discipline. Using analogies is one way of leaving such corners, of thinking the *space in-between* the different perspectives, of connecting the dots, as it were.

1.2 Metaphors / analogies / comparisons: approaches to the concept of "pharmacology"

Metaphors and analogies, however, are usually considered to be unscientific. The fact that A is, in a specific regard, similar to B, does not tell us anything about the exact qualities of either A or B. On the contrary, it could be argued that analogical thinking is the opposite of logical thinking. In many cases it is a paranoid mode of thinking that sees similarities and connections everywhere. In some cases, these uncontrolled analogies and comparisons have severe consequences: "Metaphors can kill" — this was the pointed diagnosis of cognitive linguist George Lakoff in a critical essay on the military involvement of the Americans in the Gulf region in 1991.[7] For Lakoff metaphors are not simply a decorative accessory to figurative speech, but rather shape our way of perceiving the world and our thinking, in making possible the understanding of one conceptual domain in terms of another. Among a variety of metaphors used by the US administration to justify a military intervention, Lakoff

---

7   The text was originally published in *Cognitive Semiotics* (4:2, 2013, pp. 5–19). We cite from a revised version: Lakoff, George: "Metaphor and War: The Metaphor System Used to Justify War in the Gulf", in: Martin Pütz (Ed.), Thirty Years of Linguistic Evolution. Studies in honour of René Dirven on the occasion of his 60th birthday, Philadelphia/Amsterdam: John Benjamins 1992, pp. 463–482.

puts emphasis on a "common metaphor in which military control by the enemy is seen as a *cancer* that can spread. In this metaphor, military 'operations' by friendly powers are seen as hygienic measures to 'clean out' enemy fortifications. Bombing raids are portrayed as 'surgical strikes' to 'take out' anything that can serve a military purpose. The metaphor is supported by imagery of shiny metallic instruments of war, especially jets"[8].

According to Susan Sontag, who has devoted a lengthy essay to the analysis of metaphors of illness, "[t]o describe a phenomenon as a cancer is an incitement to violence. The use of cancer in political discourse encourages fatalism and justifies 'severe' measures — as well as strongly reinforcing the widespread notion that the disease is necessarily fatal"[9]. Sontag, who wrote these lines in 1978, was not referring to the political rhetoric of the Bush Snr. administration. Her examples of the violence unleashed by the cancer metaphor are the linguistic characterizations which the Nazis inflicted on the Jews. After the Nazis had portrayed the Jews as an infection of the racial body through 'tuberculosis' and 'syphilis', they later switched to calling the Jews 'cancerous', in order to justify an increasingly harsher politico-medical treatment. The climactic series of metaphors, or so Sonntag's argument goes, led to a corresponding increase in political antidotes, from persecution to ghettoization and eventually extermination.

Metaphors that portray the political enemy as a disease — be it as a viral infection, as an infestation with parasites or as a cancerous tumor — are as common as they are problematic. And — despite the cautionary example that Nazi rhetoric still provides us with today — its use in political discourse is not diminishing. In 2003, in the run-up to America's second Gulf War, Lakoff felt compelled to write a follow-up article entitled "Metaphor and War, Again"[10].

Another failed analogy in the history of political thought is probably Heidegger's claim that the extermination of the European Jews,

---

8   Ibid., p. 472.
9   Sontag, Susan: Illness as Metaphor, New York: Vintage Books, 1978, p. 84.
10 Lakoff, George: Metaphor and War, Again. UC Berkeley 2003. Retrieved from https://escholarship.org/uc/item/32b962zb (01.02.2022).

i.e. the Holocaust, and industrial farming are "somehow" rooted in the same mindset and therefore "somehow" similar. When he declared the similarity of industrial genocide and industrial farming, he tried to blur the line between modernity in general and National-Socialist violence in particular: if somehow modernity was nothing but "forgetting being" altogether, his own involvement in National Socialism could suddenly be framed as a meaningful "fate". Heidegger is a striking example of analogical thinking getting out of control.

Against this background, it is not astounding that the distrust of analogies should have a long tradition. Plato's famous attack on rhetoric, his attempt to establish a more controlled and proper way of discussing things, the *dialektiké techné*, can be understood as an effort to overcome a way of thinking that progresses by stating similarities without really getting to the bottom of things. The phrase that "somehow" everything is like water (*pánta rhei*), for example, was an analogical statement that marked the insufficient intellectual tools of his predecessors, Plato claimed. Therefore, overcoming confusion for Plato is the same as overcoming false or uncontrolled analogies. Leaving the cave is leaving behind the delusions that wrong analogies produce in our mind. The philosophical *paideia* has to lead us from analogies to logic.

The ironic structure of this *paideia* is obvious, however: the path from analogical to logical thinking is presented in a *paradeigma*, an analogy, the myth of the cave. We can conclude that for Plato the real challenge was not to overcome analogies in general, but to control them, to use them in a skillful, elegant and productive way. This is why Plato himself became the grandmaster of philosophical myth-making, of analogies and metaphors that are still, after more than 2.000 years, a shared heritage of our culture. We overcome the unskilled way of using analogies by using other analogies skillfully.

With regard to metaphors of (political) illness, Susan Sontag shows that these are among the oldest and most powerful political metaphors of all. This has to do with the fact that the political community or the state, long before a second, technical interpretation gained plausibility with the paradigm of a mechanism, was understood as an organism, as a body — a 'body politic'. Three dimensions of meaning make this organicist metaphor suitable for thinking about politics: firstly, the 'body politic' denotes a complex unity of plurality that can be differentiated into body parts and organs, but can only become effective in interaction; secondly, the body parts are in more or less hierarchical relationships of superiority and subordination[11]; and thirdly, in the light of this interplay, it is possible to distinguish between ordered and disordered, 'healthy' and 'sick' states of the body.[12] This third dimension opens up a further field of metaphors relating to the task of the politician, who through his actions is charged with the task of maintaining the order of the body as a hierarchically structured whole. In addition to the image of the helmsman, that of the doctor or medic is one of the oldest characterizations of the politician[13]. The metaphorization of the politician as a doctor is used by Plato himself and is a recurring image throughout the history of political ideas. It serves Machiavelli in emphasizing his point that it is not moral integrity but "the ability to recognize diseases that are difficult to diagnose"[14] that constitutes the most important virtue of the politician.

A skillful and productive use of metaphors can be found in Heidegger as well. A word like "Gestell" can be helpful since it allows us to imagine a totality of imperatives. To be "gestellt" means to be stopped in one's tracks or cornered (for instance, by a fierce dog),

---

11 The body metaphor leaves room for various political interpretations. While the political theory of absolutism, for example, relies on 'localist' concepts of organism, which are based on the categorical distinction between head/body which is reconciled in the heart, the French revolutionaries refer to 'vitalistic' concepts, according to which the life of the body is sustained through the bloodstream. Cf. de Baecque, Antoine: Le corps de l'histoire. Métaphores et politique (1770–1800), Paris: Calmann-Lévy 1993, p. 119.

12 Musolff, Andreas: "Political metaphor and bodies politic", in: Urszula Okulska/Piotr Cap (Eds.), Perspectives in Politics and Discourse, Amsterdam: John Benjamins 2010, pp. 23–42, p. 25.

13 Münkler, Herfried: "Arzt und Steuermann: Metaphern des Politikers", in: Herfried Münkler (Ed.), Politische Bilder, Politik der Metaphern, Frankfurt a.M.: Fischer 1994, pp. 125–140.

14 Ibid., p. 134. All translations from non-English texts are ours.

while a "Gestell" is a structure or frame of connected imperatives, the totality of obligations and mandatory conditions surrounding us in modern society. The fact that Heidegger's use of analogies (oscillating between conceptual and metaphorical use) turns out to be fatal in some cases and helpful in others, shows the ambivalence of analogical thinking.

Metaphors and analogies therefore should not be considered as mere anomalies of thought, as signs of "wild thinking" or as mere rhetorical tricks. We could also frame them as tools which allow us to open a space of thought, to explore a field of possible, though not necessary, similarities. It is helpful, it seems, to remember what Hans Blumenberg wrote about "controlled ambiguity": it is exactly the non-binary, non-propositional, multi-valent character of the analogy which allows it to operate as an eye-opener. Not everything such "opened eyes" perceive will turn out to be true; but new aspects, new connections, new ideas are generated when unexpected comparisons are proposed.

Bernard Stiegler's term "digital pharmacology", we take it, is exactly such an explorative analogy. It opens a field of possible and supposedly fruitful comparisons. Stiegler introduces the term "digital pharmacology" in the context of his larger research project on the general concept of pharmacology.

The most striking and important aspect of this new way of looking at the interaction of the human mind and its exogenic organs is the implication that the "tools" we use are actually a lot more than tools: they enter our body and mind, they restructure our brains and our thought.

For Bernard Stiegler the importance of writing (and handwriting) and reading is the most evident and empirically explored example. The practice of reading and writing "format" our being, they change the way the human being thinks, lives, and feels. Foucault's text about "Writing the Self"[15] was crucial to Stiegler, but what makes Stiegler so outstanding as a philosopher is his deep interest in contemporary empirical research. Notably Maryanne

---

15 Foucault, Michel: "L'écriture de soi", in: Dits et écrits, Paris: Gallimard (Quarto) 2001, t. II, n° 329.

Wolf[6], with her "science of the reading brain", allowed him to underscore his point: the human being thinks not only with the brain, but also with books, with pens, with all the *pharmaka* he or she uses. It is important to emphasize that for Stiegler, the term *pharmakon* was not just an analogy or a metaphor: the *pharmakon* of the book actually, *literally*, impacts our brains, it is not *like* a *pharmakon*, but it actually *is* a *pharmakon*.

The real sense in which digital media can become *pharmaka* is shown by the fact that excessive internet-use nowadays is not only referred to as "internet addiction", but is sometimes actually treated like a severe form of physical drug addiction.[17] On the basis of neurophysiological findings,[18] the distinction between 'hard' dependence on chemical substances and 'soft' dependence on habits such as internet use is actually collapsing: "emerging evidence points to 'strong neural similarities' that effectively deconstruct the distinction [...] between 'physical' and 'psychological' addiction [...], meaning that the dopamine system can be programmed by technology just as much as Class A drugs"[19].

In order to use the fruitful term "digital pharmacology" as an explorative analogy, as an idea which opens a field of reflection, we will, in this paper, try to reconstruct und think further Stiegler's coining of the term. We will proceed in three steps: in a first step we will reconstruct the thought figure of pharmacology in a thinker who most thoroughly penetrated the pharmacological structure of

---

16   Wolf, Maryanne: Proust and the Squid. The Story and Science of the Reading Brain, New York: Harper Perennial 2008.

17   For a systematic review of the pharmacological literature see Przepiorka, Aneta/Małgorzata, Blachnio/Miziak, Agata/Czuczwar, Barbara/Jerzy, Stanisław: "Clinical approaches to treatment of Internet addiction", in: Pharmacological Reports 66 (2014), pp. 187–191.

18   See Mosher, Dave: "High Wired: Does Addictive Internet Use Restructure the Brain?", in: Scientific American (2011), https://www.scientificamerican.com/article/does-addictive-internet-use-restructure-brain/ (01.02.2022).

19   Moore, Gerald: "The pharmacology of addiction", in: Parrhesia 29 (2018), pp. 190–211, p. 197.

the pre-digital world, without using the term *pharmakon*, but employing related metaphors in the field of medicine: Rousseau.

Stiegler systematically refers to Rousseau as a "transcendental" anthropologist, who has brought to light the "aporia of origin".[20] There are considerable parallels between the two, which suggest that Rousseau can be interpreted as a pharmacological thinker (in the double sense of the word). Firstly, like Stiegler, Rousseau also sees contemporary society plagued by numerous pathologies which he attributes to the influx of technological and cultural innovations. Illness, however, is not something accidental that can be separated from the human condition. Rather, and this is the second parallel, man is essentially a pharmacological being himself. Thirdly, promising means of healing have to take this pharmacological constellation into account; they have to conceive of (self-)education as auto-pharmacology. With Rousseau as an example, it can be shown in what sense the post-metaphysical condition of modernity opens the field to pharmacology.

In a second step we will discuss to what extent Stiegler's idea of a *digital* pharmacology goes beyond Rousseau's general pharmacological analysis, with which — as already indicated — it has remarkable similarities. Our aim is to show to what extent Stiegler's concept of "grammatization" is a key term for analyzing the digital media technology present in a given context.

In a third step we will try to do something that Bernard Stiegler himself would probably have refused to do: we would like to push the idea of "digital pharmacology" to its limits, rendering explicit the implications the term seems to contain. After all, if Bernard Stiegler was right to claim that smartphones, computers, smartwatches and tablets are best understood as *pharmaka* flooding our world, it seems evident that our way of dealing with such *pharmaka* might profit from our experience with non-digital *pharmaka*.

---

20   Stiegler, Bernard: Technics and time, 1. The fault of Epimetheus. Transl Richard Beardsworth and George Collins, Stanford: Stanford University Press 1998, pp. 82ff. On Stiegler's reading of Rousseau, see Roberts, Ben "Rousseau, Stiegler and the aporia of origin", in: Forum for Modern Language Studies 42 (2006), pp. 382–394.

In order to do this, we propose, first of all, to consider pharmacology as a political activity: dealing (in the double sense) with *pharmaka* is a social practice. The law defines the parameters, the rules of engagement, and the ways in which *pharmaka* are produced, distributed, consumed, mixed and viewed. Pharmacology is not just a scientific endeavor, an attempt to understand the complex causalities at work when we use chemical or biological substances. Politics understood as the *practice of establishing collectively binding decisions*, also decides about what we drink, smoke, or inject. This is why different societies have developed very different cultures of pharmacology.

It might be helpful to distinguish a level of *explicit rules*, i.e. the laws defining what substances are categorized as recreational drugs, what substances are viewed as medicine and what is considered just a kind of food. We are, at the moment, witnessing major changes in our pharmacological governmentality, as more and more countries start to legalize cannabis. However, governmentality also implied for Foucault all the implicit rules, all the ways in which different things are valued or framed. Drinking champagne is different from drinking beer, just as smoking expensive Cuban cigars is different from smoking cheap cigarettes. Pharmacology is therefore not only a political matter in the sense of an *explicit* policy, but also in the sense of an *implicit* culture, a social consensus.

If we take into account both the explicit and the implicit level, the important consequence consists in overcoming the paradigm of pharmacology as an individual task: Of course, every human being has a responsibility to use *pharmaka* in an intelligent way. However, if we frame pharmacology (with Stiegler) in the general sense as a social practice, we can conclude that the parameters of the way we interact with *pharmaka* are not within the realm of our individual horizon: only a culture, a social network can establish and transfer the art of writing and reading. Wittgenstein claimed that there could not be a fully private language: and in the same way we state that there cannot be a private pharmacology.

This is also why Stiegler emphasized with great zeal the importance of intergenerational transmission: it is crucial that not every generation should have to repeat the mistakes of its predecessors.

The objects of the "third retention", i.e. culturally stored knowledge, were therefore in the focus of Stiegler' attention: books in particular allow cultures to transfer knowledge and experience across generations. What is taught, how it is taught, to whom it is taught — all these questions are decided on in a political context. Pharmacology is therefore always already embedded in a "politics of pharmacology".

Chapter 2: Pharmacology on the Threshold of Modernity: Rousseau

2.1 Illness as social pathology

The term pharmacology originally comes from the semantic field of disease. The metaphor of illness, however, is a controversial and ambiguous figure of speech in political theory. For this reason, it seems appropriate to deal more fundamentally with the imagery of illness in politics. The aforementioned Susan Sontag differentiates between two sickness metaphors, ancient and modern: the ancient notion holds that "[t]reatment is aimed at restoring the right balance — in political terms, the right hierarchy"[1]. This understanding, which according to Sontag was widespread from Plato to Hobbes, was eventually replaced in 18th century political discourse by a 'modern' metaphor of illness: "The modern idea of revolution, based on an estimate of the unremitting bleakness of the existing political situation, shattered the old, optimistic use of disease metaphors"[2]. The French Revolution undermined the confidence that political grievances can be cured by old and proven remedies. It is not that the revolutionaries did not try this — as Hannah Arendt argues, they themselves initially misunderstood the revolutionary overcoming of the old order as its restoration[3] — but the recipes failed and gradually a new image of health took

---

1 S. Sontag: Illness as Metaphor, p. 75.
2 S. Sontag: Illness as Metaphor, p. 80.
3 Arendt, Hannah: On Revolution (orig. 1963), London: Faber & Faber 2016, ch. 1.

hold that was linked to the idea of overcoming the disease through a new beginning, a process of *régénération* [4], as the revolutionary discourse would have it. The radicalism of this new way of thinking is reflected in the political use of the most prominent medical metaphor of the era. In the case of Abbé Sieyès, who wrote a kind of "script"[5] for the Revolution with his appeal to the third estate, the nobility is defamed as a 'parasitic caste', as a 'cancer' that can only be cured by 'amputation'.[6]

Sontag's description of a change in the use of disease metaphors in the political discourse of the 18th century is visionary and underpinned by many plausible observations; yet it has a normative dimension which is less convincing. She considers this new sickness metaphor, which expresses "a sense of dissatisfaction with society as such"[7], to be inherently dangerous, because it tends to unleash violence. This becomes clear when she draws a direct connection from the revolutionary thought to the totalitarianism of the 20th century:

> It is hardly the last time that revolutionary violence would be justified on the grounds that society has a radical, horrible illness. [...] Modern totalitarian movements, whether of the right or of the left, have been peculiarly — and revealingly — inclined to use disease imagery[8].

Let us exclude, for a moment, the normative qualification and stick to Sontag's descriptive capture of a change from classical to modern disease metaphors in political discourse. Several aspects can be distinguished in this regard. First, the classical concept of political sickness relates to a momentary tendency to decline or an acute

---

4 Ozouf, Mona: "Régénération", in: François Furet/Mona Ozouf (Eds.), Dictionnaire critique de la Révolution française, Paris: Flammarion 1988, pp. 821–831; see also Ozouf, Mona: L'homme régénéré. Essai sur la Révolution française, Paris: Gallimard 1989.
5 Sewell, William H.: A Rhetoric of Bourgeois Revolution. The Abbé Sieyes and What is the Third Estate?, Durham: Duke University Press 1994, p. 53.
6 A. de Baecque: Le corps de l'histoire, p. 110.
7 S. Sontag: Illness as Metaphor, p. 73.
8 Ibid., p. 82.

state of disorder; health, as a well-ordered state, is assumed to be unproblematic and a generally agreed-upon condition. By contrast, modern disease metaphors signify more systemic processes, which seem to be fundamentally intertwined with the general evolution of society. "[W]hat is at issue is health itself"[9]. Second, whereas sickness in the classical conception is purely a metaphorical attribute of the 'body politic', in the modern account the disease makes itself felt in individual suffering, which manifests itself in a discomfort or unease on the part of the social actors, who feel, but do not really grasp what is going wrong.

> [T]he modern metaphors suggest a profound disequilibrium between individual and society, with society conceived as the individual's adversary. [Modern] [d]isease metaphors are used to judge society not as out of balance but as repressive[10].

Third, this systemic character of the disease consequently leads to a decrease in the previous trust in healing through statecraft. As a consequence, healing seems either utopian, or possible only through radical means like a permanent regeneration.

While Sonntag focuses on the third, curative, aspect from which she deduces the dangerousness of modern disease metaphors, it is worth taking a closer look at the first two, more diagnostic, aspects. Here a discourse shift becomes clear that could be described as a transition from the concept of political sickness to that of social pathology. Frederick Neuhouser has worked out this difference in some detail. He characterizes a social pathology by "the idea of a practice which systematically runs counter to the ends of those who participate in this practice"[11]. The notion of 'practice' is crucial here: a practice is a result of individual actions; it is contingent in the sense that it has social, not natural, causes (a fundamental difference to classical political thought's assumption of the teleology of human action). The concept of a practice presupposes that actors

---

9   Ibid., p. 72.
10 Ibid., p. 73.
11 Neuhouser, Frederick: "Rousseau und die Idee einer 'pathologischen' Gesellschaft", in: Politische Vierteljahrsschrift 53 (2012), pp. 628–645, p. 630.

take part in it who are responsible, at least in principle, for their actions. For this reason, the diagnosis of a social pathology, which indicates that the purposes of action are thwarted, always implies an element of criticism which holds people responsible for not living up to the standards of a good life. To call a society pathological is therefore different from calling it unjust.

As a consequence of the opaque nature of a social pathology, the healthy and the unhealthy states of a society can no longer be kept strictly apart (as in the classical model): on the contrary, they are deeply intermingled, conceptual twins, as it were. The history of society is the history of its deprivation. This idea is the *leitmotif* of the social philosophy of Jean-Jacques Rousseau, whom Neuhouser calls the father of the idea of a pathological society, an idea that was influential among 19th century social philosophers like Hegel, Durkheim and Nietzsche[12]. Rousseau, however, is particularly interesting as the interface between the classical and the modern understanding of political illness. He is the first political thinker to base his social philosophy and political theory on the diagnosis of a social pathology, and one of the last to take up the tradition of conceptualizing politics as a potential 'cure' by analogy with medicine.

Rousseau has a special and conflict-ridden relationship with the medicine of his time; numerous references can be found in his autobiographical, educational, socio-philosophical and political writings. At first glance he appears to be a dedicated critic of medicine, harshly slamming the "rule of the art of medicine, an art which is in any case more dangerous to people than all the evils that it claims to be able to cure"[13]. His polemics are particularly true of the self-misunderstanding of medicine as a science that devotes great care and energy to description and classification. In contrast, Rousseau emphasizes: "The only really useful part of the science of medicine is the art of hygiene; moreover, it is less of a science than a virtue"[14].

---

12   Ibid., p. 628.
13   Rousseau, Jean-Jacques: Collection complète des œuvres de Jean-Jacques Rousseau, 17 volumes, Genève 1780–1789, vol. IV, p. 37.
14   Ibid., p. 40.

The biographical background cannot be overlooked. Because of his unstable state of health, Rousseau consulted numerous doctors between 1732 and 1736[15], and found that the majority of them either did not have sufficient knowledge of his ailment, or at least could not make a clear, precise diagnosis of it. After an odyssey of various examinations and futile attempts to find appropriate treatment, Rousseau draws the personal conclusion that he should allow himself "to recover or to die without doctors and remedies"[16].

Rousseau's complaint about the dilettantism of doctors reflects an unease with the medicine of his time that was widespread during the Enlightenment: a case in point, for example, is Molière's mockery of medics as money-tailoring charlatans in his *zeitgeist*-invoking play "The Imaginary Invalid" (Le Malade Imaginaire). With Rousseau, however, this criticism takes a specific socio-critical turn. For him, the real causes of illness are of a social nature, so "that one could easily write the history of human illness by following that of our civilized society"[17].

How does Rousseau justify the view that the history of human disease is inextricably linked with the history of civilization? — For him the concept of illness is closely related to that of unnaturalness. Civilization, through which people leave their 'state of nature', means falling away from a 'natural way of life'. Rousseau cites as an example the change in eating habits, "the overly artificial dishes of the rich, which nourish them with hot juices and burden them with digestive disorders", and on the other hand "the meagre food of the poor, which they are mostly still lacking and the lack of which leads them to greedily overload their stomachs when the opportunity arises"[18]. It becomes clear that Rousseau explains denaturation not naturalistically, but culturally; for him it is about a change in the habits of eating (not primarily about the food itself).

This is underlined by other examples of the artificial way of life in civilization, "the waking nights, the debauchery of every kind,

---

15   J. J. Rousseau: Collection complète des œuvres, vol. X, pp. 303ff.
16   J. J. Rousseau: Collection complète des œuvres, vol. XVI, p. 167.
17   J. J. Rousseau: Collection complète des œuvres, vol. I, p. 53.
18   Ibid.

[...] the worries and hardships without number [...]: these are the ominous evidence that most of our sufferings are our own work"[19]. At the end of his detailed list, which reads like a sweeping attack on the decadence of contemporary urban society, Rousseau sums up his understanding of illness as unnatural: he writes "that the state of reflection is a state against nature and that the man who thinks is a degenerate animal"[20].

In the light of such lines, Voltaire scoffed at Rousseau in his reply that one felt like walking on all fours. But if we leave the cultural pessimism aside, it becomes clear that Rousseau understands illness structurally as a state of imbalance between desire and its potential satisfaction. As Rousseau explains in "Emile", nature gives man "first of all only the desires necessary for his preservation and the abilities sufficient to fulfill them. [...] Only in the original state are forces and desires in balance."[21] The health of humans in the 'natural state' consists in the fact that their desires (e.g. hunger) come to a halt spontaneously in satisfaction (e.g. the consumption of a fruit) (Second Discourse, p. 67). They are not yet worried by the hunger of tomorrow[22], i.e. they are not yet providential beings. Illness, on the other hand, is the state of falling away from this state of momentary happiness. It is triggered by the awakening of the imagination, which produces a state of differential desire.

Jacques Derrida[23] has worked out this self-reinforcing dynamic of unattainability, which is characteristic of Rousseau's thinking and which is constituted by the imaginative representation of the absent. As soon as the fragile state of equilibrium has been disturbed by the awakening of the imagination, the "natural" balance between desire and restraint turns out to be an "impossible

---

19   Ibid.
20   Ibid.
21   J.-J. Rousseau: Collection complète des œuvres, vol. IV, p. 89.
22   Hobbes, Thomas: De cive, ed. Howard Warrender, Oxford: Clarendon Press 1983, ch. 10.
23   Derrida, Jacques: De la Grammatologie. Paris: Editions de Minuit 1967, p. 262ff.

balance"²⁴. In Rousseau's own words: "The imagination expands for us [...] the measure of the possible and consequently arouses and nourishes the desires through the hope to satisfy them. But the goal that you seemed to be reaching flees faster than you can pursue it."²⁵ Through the development of the imagination, the needs grow exponentially, the desire becomes excessive, or, to stick with the medical imagery, "feverish"²⁶.

2.2 Rousseau and the genesis of modern self-medication

Does Rousseau's conception of the process of civilization allow anything other than the pessimistic conclusion that health is irretrievably lost, and that our pathological society is consequently a habitat that we cannot escape? If one looks only at the "Second Discourse" with its culturally pessimistic thrust, then this reading suggests an inevitable pathogenesis of human civilization. In contrast, Derrida and other interpreters have shown convincingly that in Rousseau the terms nature/culture or healthy/sick are not to be thought of independently of one another and cannot be assigned separately to any particular historical periods or stages in the development of humankind.

For Derrida, nature in its double meaning as a biological foundation and as a normative ideal is a term that cannot be conceived without its "supplement", culture²⁷. Like health, nature is a *liminal term*. "It is not a question of leaving nature, nor of returning to it, but rather of diminishing its 'being distant'."²⁸

Given this supplementary structure, how is healing to be imagined? Rousseau hints at homeopathic therapy according to the prin-

---

24 J.Derrida: Grammatologie, p. 265.
25 J.-J. Rousseau: Collection complète des œuvres, vol. IV, p. 89.
26 Cited after F. Neuhouser: Rousseau und die Idee einer 'pathologischen' Gesellschaft, p. 637ff.
27 J. Derrida: Grammatologie, p. 255.
28 Ibid. p. 264.

ciple *similia similibus curentur*: "Eternal providence, by placing salutary simples alongside noxious plants, and by endowing the substance of certain harmful animals with remedies for their wounds, has taught the sovereigns who are its ministers to imitate its wisdom"[29]. Jean Starobinski made this the main theme of an essay entitled "The Antidote in the Poison: The Thought of Jean-Jacques Rousseau". He brilliantly shows that for Rousseau the homeopathic formula, far from being a principle confined to medicine proper, serves as a universal key to understanding the apparently paradoxical in the structure of his (i.e. Rousseau's) own thought. The arts and sciences, which Rousseau accuses in his "First Discourse" of degrading or even perverting the human species, are both poison and cure: literary writing is corrupting *and* cultivating, the theater has both isolating *and* communalizing effects. The same structure also permeates Rousseau's political thought. The social contract demands complete alienation, but is, *as such*, a liberating act. What all these different examples have in common is the fact that the "intervention of a therapist [...] is required to extract the remedy from the poison"[30].

Starobinski's essay has received widespread reception. However, his metaphor of homeopathy has not established itself as a leading concept in the Rousseau interpretation.[31] This may be due to

---

29 Starobinski, Jean: "The Antidote in the Poison: The Thought of Jean-Jacques Rousseau", in: Jean Starobinski (Ed.), Blessings in Disguise; or, the Morality of Evil, Transl. Arthur Goldhammer, Cambridge: Harvard UP 1993, pp. 118–168, p. 119.

30 J. Starobinski: The Antidote in the Poison, p. 120.

31 Neuhouser takes up the medical metaphor when he reconstructs Rousseau's social philosophy under the terms 'diagnosis', 'prescription' and 'curing the malady' — but he does not explicitly use the terms 'homeopathic' or 'pharmacological'. See Neuhouser, Frederick: Rousseau's Theodicy of Self-Love. Evil, Rationality, and the Drive for Recognition, New York: Oxford UP 2008. — An exception is Bottici, who uses homeopathy and pharmacology interchangeably. Bottici, Chiara: "Democracy and the spectacle: On Rousseau's homeopathic strategy", in: Philosophy and Social Criticism 41 (2015), pp. 235–248.

the fact that this image is so pertinent in Rousseau's writings, that the term *metaphor* does not seem fitting enough to capture its centrality. Maria Gullstam assumes Starobinski's stance of Rousseau, but replaces the term "homeopathy" by Derrida's concept of '*pharmakon*', which seems better suited to characterize a "thought structure [which] is indeed present in Rousseau's philosophy on a level that reaches beyond the recurring remedy/poison metaphor"[32]. In his text "Plato's Pharmacy", Derrida reveals a characteristic structure of occidental thought, which is based on the superiority of the spoken word over written language. This basic idea is analyzed in a close reading of Plato's work *Phaedrus*. The point of Derrida's deconstruction is that Plato's argument that only spoken language is capable of reaching the sphere of ideas is not tenable on closer reading. Derrida reveals the view as a subtext in Plato that written and oral use of language always refer to one another and cannot be separated — just as the Greek term '*pharmakon*' encompasses the opposing meanings of poison and cure.

It does not seem problematic to transfer this structure back to Rousseau. The text "Plato's Pharmacy" serves as a further explanation of Derrida's basic idea in "Grammatology" that the meaning of texts is interwoven with a supplementary logic, which he had demonstrated using Rousseau's use of the term 'nature'. To this extent, Rousseau's metaphor of homeopathic healing is a pharmacological image *par excellence*.

With a view to Rousseau' anthropology, it does not seem exaggerated to call man a pharmacological animal. On the one hand, unlike in the harmonistic doctrines of the natural law tradition, no *telos* exists for Rousseau that would channel and control the development of society through a social instinct inherent in human beings. On the other hand, however, Rousseau also criticizes the 'realistic' anthropology of Hobbes, who traces human nature back to some supposedly universal laws of motion and understands human

---

[32] Gullstam, Maria: Rousseau's Idea of Theatre. From Criticism to Practice, Doctoral Thesis in Theatre Studies at Stockholm University, Sweden 2020, http://www.diva-portal.org/smash/get/diva2:1430104/FULLTEXT01.pdf.

behavior as a vector of appetitive and aversive strivings, an analysis which results in the famous formula of man being man's wolf. The first view is naive because it presupposes a pre-established harmony between self-love and the social whole; the second is unhistorical because it hypostheizes a certain gestalt of human self-love which, as Rousseau strives to demonstrate, came into being only with bourgeois competitive society[33]. Both of these perspectives fail to recognize the essential pharmacological structure of human self-love.

In Rousseau's description of man in the state of nature, self-love plays a prominent role; it is the seed of an arsenal of emotions and passions that can develop from it: "The source of our passions and the origin of all others is self-love that comes with the man's birth and which does not leave him as long as he lives. It is the original passion, innate and before everything else."[34]

In the state of nature, i.e. before the awakening of the imagination through the permanent representation of our needs, the hunger of tomorrow is not yet felt and the neighbor not yet a potential competitor. Thus, the radius of self-love is limited to the immediate needs; and if there is occasional competition with others, natural pity, *pitié naturelle*, the "innate reluctance to see one's own kind suffer", moderates the desire for self-preservation and, where possible, prevents a potential escalation of ego-related motives. It is pity which "moderates the effectiveness of self-love and therefore contributes to the mutual preservation of the entire species"[35]. Man has pity as a natural gift, although this does not lead to communalization, but only asserts itself as an impulse in the event of a chance encounter with others. Pity is not an 'active potency' (*entelecheia*) which drives the realization of a given target state by itself, if it is not prevented from doing so by adverse and unusual circumstances. According to Rousseau, a family structure is not natural either, and like all interactions, mating behavior is also random and

---

33 J.-J. Rousseau: Collection complète des œuvres, vol. I, p. 73.
34 J.-J. Rousseau: Collection complète des œuvres, vol. IV, p. 360.
35 J.-J. Rousseau: Collection complète des œuvres, vol. I, p. 77.

does not lead to permanent ties[36]. Both faculties, self-love and natural compassion, stabilize a liminal state of peaceful coexistence, i.e. the state of nature, which is stationary and without history.

As part of a conjectural history of human civilization, at the beginning of the second part of the "Second Discourse", Rousseau outlines an ensemble of external causes that gradually disequilibrate this state of affairs: these include increased productivity, population growth, division of labor, private property and individualization. This external development is accompanied by the training and expansion of the faculty of the imagination, which broadens the temporal and social horizon and subsequently 'inflames' human passions. Self-love (*amour de soi*) changes to self-respect (*amour propre*), natural pity to a comparison-based form of intersubjectivity.

Amour propre has long been interpreted in Rousseau's reception as a cipher for decadence and moral decline, as a signature of advancing civilization. This interpretation is suggested not only through the predominant tone of the "Second Discourse", but also by the conceptual history of the term. The original context of the meaning of *amour propre* is theological; it is understood in Jansenism, a specific French version of Augustinianism, as self-referential love and vain selfishness — in short: as a synonym for sin. In contrast to the spontaneity of love for God, the state of sin is characterized for the Jansenists by man's reflection on his own individuality[37].

Rousseau makes use of the conceptual duality of spontaneous and reflected love, elaborated in the theological context, but does not adopt its associated fixed, normative meaning. Rather, he understands *amour propre* pharmacologically as an essential principle of civilized man which has potential consequences in both directions, good as well as bad: "As soon as the dormant forces become active, the imagination, the most lively element of all, awakens and

---

36   Ibid., p. 87ff.
37   Spaemann, Robert: Reflexion und Spontanität. Studien über Fénelon, Stuttgart: Klett-Cotta 1990, p. 188.

hurries ahead of them. The imagination expands for us, be it good or bad, the measure of the possible [...]."[38]

This structural openness of *amour propre* — or its pharmacological texture — was first stressed by the seminal interpretation of Nicholas Dent[39], who interprets *amour propre* as a basic anthropological need for social recognition. In line with this view, Neuhouser has put forward the most comprehensive interpretation of Rousseau's social philosophy, which he characterizes as a "theodicy of self-love"[40]: "Despite its essentially secular und naturalistic presuppositions, the structure of Rousseau's account mirrors that of the traditional Christian conception of human history: an original harmony among humans, God, and the world is ruptured by a fall from grace — an effect of human freedom — that corrupts human nature and initiates an era of evil and misery, but also brings with it the possibility of redemption and transcendence"[41]. Self-love in the gestalt of *amour propre* is at the same time the source of evil and the possibility of its cure; the remedy, however, cannot be taken for granted as a function of a natural teleology and not even as a kind of 'cunning of reason'. Rousseau's outlook is more modest and more humble, as Neuhouser makes clear with recourse to a Kantian reading of Rousseau:

> Rousseau's theodicy offers practical orientation. [...] [T]he goal of freedom and social harmony are not intrinsically contradictory nor in principle unachievable, Rousseau's account of evil shows that if we can have no guarantee of there being a way out of our present fallenness, we can also not know *a priori* that no such path exists[42].

---

38 J.-J. Rousseau: Collection complète des œuvres, vol. IV, p. 89.
39 Dent, Nicholas J.H.: Rousseau. An Introduction to his Psychological, Social and Political Theory, Oxford: Blackwell Publishers 1988; Dent, Nicholas J.H./O'Hagan, Timothy: "Rousseau on Amour propre", in: Proceedings of the Aristotelian Society 72 (1998), pp. 57–75.
40 F. Neuhouser: Rousseau's Theodicy of Self-Love.
41 F. Neuhouser: Rousseau's Theodicy of Self-Love, p. 2f.
42 Ibid., p. 8.

The de-pathologization of social relationships and self-relationship depends on the development of 'reasonable' needs, which cannot be nourished unchecked by the excessive power of the imagination. The central means for this are, firstly, a responsive form of education that remedies the harmful influences of society on individual development as far as possible, and, secondly, the political shaping of social conditions that enable successful recognition relationships, including, for example, the prevention of overly serious economic dependencies or the institutionalization of socially acceptable measures of distinction through e.g. political honors, etc. From the numerous measures that Rousseau is considering as possible remedies, two examples are selected below: the practice of self-education through writing as a possibility of a pharmacological analysis of subjectivity, and the institution of the theater as the object of a pharmacological analysis of social intersubjectivity.

2.3 Homeopathic self-medication: self-education through writing?

The aim of education is to socialize the individual in a sensible way; but this only appears to be possible, given Rousseau's diagnosis of civilization, if the pupil is largely shielded from the harmful influence of society in his early development phase. This task falls to the educator, who has to dose the influence of society pharmacologically. As in his social philosophy, Rousseau also uses the concept of nature as a starting-point and normative guideline in his pedagogical considerations. His treatise "Emile" aims to reconstruct the development of 'natural' man[43]. Rousseau defines as natural, analogous to his argument in the "Second Discourse", all those human qualities that an individual would develop if he did not come into contact with society. All these properties can be either "true" or "imaginary"[44]. The latter refers to the influence of the imagination,

---

43   J.-J. Rousseau: Collection complète des œuvres, vol. IV, p. 4.
44   J.-J. Rousseau: Collection complète des œuvres, vol. IV, p. 265.

which in the individual represents the influence of society, its views and prejudices.

From this guideline to shield the 'harmful' influence of society, all other educational maxims result: Emile's development should proceed as slowly as possible, which above all means carefully guiding the expansion of the world through the imagination. For this purpose, all interpersonal contacts, with the exception of the one with the educator, must be postponed as long as possible. The purpose of shielding the pupil from other people is not just to delay the awakening of the sex drive: more fundamentally the aim is to protect the pupil from the influence of the will of others. This maxim is of such fundamental importance that it is even transferred to the pedagogical relationship between educator and pupil: Emile is to learn by gaining experience, not by obeying the master's will, be it by force or by insight through conviction: "true education is less prescriptive than practical". Nonetheless, the 'experiences' that Emile has are anything but coincidental. Rather, in order to enable 'natural development', these must be 'artificially' arranged by the educator.

Like the process of civilization, the development of the individual seems to be pharmacological through and through. A self-determined life, which is the aim of education, is only possible through strategic manipulation on the part of the educator, who has to mask his intervention as if it were unfolding naturally. This analysis seems to reveal that the development of autonomy is in principle only possible as a function of (benevolent-minded) heteronomy — a structure that finds its analogy in Rousseau's political philosophy in the figure of the *législateur*, who can bring freedom to a political community through a constitution only as an outsider.[45]

Is something like self-education even conceivable under these conditions? — The possibility of self-education seems to presuppose that we can enter into a relationship of hetero-autonomous control with ourselves. A prerequisite for such a relationship to oneself is a form of reflexivity that observes the original and mutually constitutive relationship between external and self-determination in one's own biography. In his lectures on the history of sexuality, Foucault

---

45   J.-J. Rousseau: Collection complète des œuvres, vol. I, p. 232.

showed how the modern individual is shaped through a form of work on the self, and also suggested that modern biographical literature is a form of 'technique of the self': "The confession is a ritual of discourse in which the speaking subject is also the subject of the statement"[46].

Rousseau's "Confessions" can be read in this sense. Here the biographical constellation of external and self-determination is unfolded in a narrative way that enables the self to interpret its development reflexively[47]. The interrelationship of heteronomy and autonomy is thematized in the Confessions on different levels: the self can first be experienced as an authentic subject through demarcation from others and society; its 'authenticity', however, proves to be fragile and corrupted by social influence right down to the innermost impulses; as a result, the "dividing strategy"[48], through which the subject found himself in isolation from society, is applied in relation to himself, which leads to a series of differentiations between outside and inside, understanding and sensuality, feeling and passion, etc., which only ever brings to light the impossibility of finding a natural place beyond social influence. The fact that writing always addresses a (fictional) reader reveals at the same time that the self-analysis is a justifying presentation of the self in relation to the gaze of the stranger. In the process of writing this gaze is more or less internalized, and becomes a condition of the constitution of a subject.

In the more recent discourse in cultural history, the practice of reading and writing and their effect on the subjectivity of the bourgeois subject have received a lot of attention. In his genealogy of modern subject cultures, Andreas Reckwitz devotes a separate paragraph to the creation of "bourgeois inwardness in the medium

---

46 Foucault, Michel: The History of Sexuality, Volume I: An Introduction, New York: Pantheon 1978, p. 61.

47 Gutman, Huck: "Rousseau's Confessions: A Technology of the Self", in: Michel Foucault/Luther H. Martin/Huck Gutman/Patrick H. Hutton (Eds.), Technologies of the Self. A Seminar with Michel Foucault, Amherst: University of Massachusetts Press 1988, pp. 99–120.

48 H. Gutman: Rousseau's Confessions, p. 108.

of writing"[49]. For him, reading and writing are the cultural practices that create the self-controlled, autonomous subject capable of morality assumed by the Enlightenment: "The subject educated in reading carries out an unconscious self-government of physical movements, a permanent concentration of attention."[50]

While Reckwitz primarily traces the 'inward', self-disciplining and focusing effect of reading and writing, Lynn Hunt reconstructs their social 'external' effects. According to her interpretation, it was only a culture of letter and novel writing with a focus on the inner states of individuals which created the psycho-social basis for the mutual perception of human beings as equals with regard to their shared vulnerability and their common need for recognition. The emergence of the new genres of biographical literature and the epistolary novel, which had the development of inner life as its main theme, played a decisive role in the change in subjectivity that would ultimately also bring about human rights: "[R]eading novels created a sense of equality and empathy through passionate involvement in the narrative"[51].

Nevertheless, looking back at Rousseau, it is difficult to fully appreciate the positive aspects of the bourgeois culture of inwardness. For him, reading and writing are *pharmaka* that, as remedies, are also poisons. The reflection of the inner state can be authentic *and* vain, the participation in the suffering of others can result from sympathy *and* voyeuristic curiosity — there will always be a mixture, the proportions of which can never be adequately determined by either the outside onlooker or the self-observer. What can be determined with certainty, however, is that the observation of self and other is a structural trait of bourgeois society.

---

[49] Reckwitz, Andreas: Das hybride Subjekt. Eine Theorie der Subjektkulturen von der bürgerlichen Moderne zur Postmoderne, Weilerswist: Velbrück Wissenschaft 2006, pp. 155f.

[50] A. Reckwitz: Das hybride Subjekt, p. 160.

[51] Hunt, Lynn: Inventing Human Rights. A History, New York (NY)/London: Norton 2007, p. 39.

2.4 Culture as a homeopathic remedy: civic education through the theater?

Just as the literary genres of biographical writing are discussed in 18th century Enlightenment discourse as a medium of possible self-education, as a playing field for an imagination that refines itself in the interior of the psyche, so a debate also arises in the field of playwriting and drama theory as to whether the institution of the theater is a possible place of civic education, a social playing field for the cultivation of the imagination. Rousseau is also directly involved in this discourse. In his "Letter to d'Alembert" he sharply criticizes the author of the article about his hometown Geneva for the *Encyclopédie*, in which d'Alembert recommended that the Swiss provincial city introduce a theater based on the Parisian model. D'Alembert argued that the establishment of a modern theater could contribute to the cultural refinement of the customs of Geneva and, consequently, could be a component of a program of civic education. According to d'Alembert the theater "would form the taste of the citizens and would give them a fineness of tact, a delicacy of sentiments"[52]. Not only the performances themselves were to contribute to this, but also the fact that with the settlement of actors and directors in Geneva a new social class would be established which would bring with it a certain cultural growth through its presence in city life. The theater would therefore be something like a nucleus of modernization in old-fashioned and provincial Geneva.

Rousseau responds to this suggestion with a criticism that at first sight is devastating, but on closer view turns out to be a pharmacological analysis of theatricality as a principle of modern bourgeois society. His numerous invectives and polemics can be grouped into two strands of criticism: Rousseau's first argument against the theater is that acting is based on the art of pretense, to a certain extent on a professional form of hypocrisy that removes people from truth and authenticity. This argument is reminiscent of Plato's criticism of poetry as a representation of appearances and not truth, but has a specifically contemporary thrust. In Enlightenment theater

---

52 Cited after M. Gullstam: Rousseau's Idea of Theatre, p. 91.

discourse, the question was discussed as to whether the feelings of the character to be represented by the actor should be empathized with or only externally displayed — whether the theater should be based on the image of 'emotional acting' or 'reflective acting'. Denis Diderot, a leading figure of the Paris Enlightenment, editor of the *Encyclopédie* (and thus the figure in the background of d'Alembert's article), and himself a playwright, rejected the maxim of sensitive empathy as a condition of acting in his reflections on the theater. Rather, the actor should be constantly aware of the split between his personality and the character he is portraying.

For Rousseau, this definition of acting as the art of disguise is nothing more than a legitimation of hypocrisy, reminiscent of a culture of pretense and appearances, which characterized court society. Through the principle of *bienséance*, according to which the figures in a play should abide strictly by the framework of good taste and moral norms, this code of conduct entered drama theory and shaped the plays of French *classicisme*. Diderot adheres to this principle, his transformation of the *tragédie classique* to the *drame sérieux* notwithstanding. In keeping with this tradition, d'Alembert also subscribes in his article to the principles of classical decorum which Genevan society should aspire to and maintain.

Rousseau, by contrast, fears that the actor will not be able to completely give up his role when he leaves the stage and, as an exposed personality, will bring into Geneva society the vanity and desire for pleasure that predisposes him to his profession. He sees the danger that the art of disguise will gain a foothold in Geneva society and nurture a pathological form of *amour propre*, the craving for admiration, which makes people completely dependent on the judgment of their fellow men. "[T]his art of counterfeiting, of appearing different than what we actually are, is particularly dangerous because it contains the very same dialectic between being and appearing that, according to Rousseau, is one of the greatest evils of modern society"[53].

Rousseau's first argument does not seem very convincing, however, because acting as the art of disguise is problematic and would

---

53 C. Bottici: Democracy and the spectacle, p. 239.

contaminate social interactions in 'real' life only if it were not debunked as art(-ificial). But isn't it characteristic of modern theater as a form of autonomous art that both sides of the theatrical relationship tend to become more professional: the actor as well as the audience?

In fact, Diderot ascribes an attitude of professionalized distance to the audience as well, which in a sense results from the redefinition of the role of the actor. He understands the audience as purely spectators, with whom the actors should not come into direct contact either through speech or looks. They should act, "as if the curtain did not go up"[54]. According to Diderot, this distancing has the paradoxical result that the spectator's emotional involvement in the play is increased, but in a refined way. Instead of sympathizing with the characters' emotions, they are confronted with the perception of their own aesthetic feelings — which can be better controlled, lack a tendency toward immediate action and are therefore open to moral reflection[55].

Rousseau does not find this line of argument convincing. His second argument against the theater draws on the claim attributed to Diderot that the feelings triggered in the audience by the play are purely aesthetic, which, in Rousseau's view, does not make them suitable for secondary moralization. On the contrary, they no longer constitute any social cohesion and do not create solidarity. The audience in the theater is a lonely crowd.

Regarding the theatrical emotion of compassion for the tragic hero — a leading theme in 18th century drama theory, particularly in Lessing — Rousseau argues:

> But what kind of pity is that? A fleeting and vain shock that lasts no longer than the appearance that creates it; a remnant of a natural sensation that is soon suffocated by the passions, sterile compas-

---

54 Diderot, Denis: "De la poésie dramatique", in: Denis Diderot (Ed.), Œuvres esthétiques, Paris: Garnier 1959, pp. 179–287, p. 231.
55 Kolesch, Doris: Theater der Emotionen. Ästhetik und Politik zur Zeit Ludwigs XIV, Frankfurt a.M./New York: Campus 2006, p. 237.

sion that drowns itself in its own tears and has never produced the slightest act of humanity.[56]

Because theatrical identification only serves to increase one's own pleasure, it focuses on what separates the audience and the suffering actor. In theatrical pity there is "no concern for ourselves"[57]. "The more I think about it, the clearer it becomes to me that what is presented in the theater is not being brought closer to us, but taken away from us."[58].

As in the first argument, the diagnosis is that the theater claims or encourages the imagination in a way that has socially pathological consequences. While the actor fakes foreign states of mind in order to achieve an effect in the audience, the spectator uses his imagination to understand other people's fates for the sake of his amusement — neither of the parties breaks the circle of egocentrism, either through the imaginative anticipation of other peoples's reactions to their own acts (actor), nor through the imaginative comprehension of the suffering of others (spectator).

Where is the pharmacological aspect of Rousseau's criticism of the theater, where can elements of a cure to the evil be found? Derrida's analysis of the supplementary logic of Rousseau's argument is again helpful. He elaborates on the "ambivalence of the imagination" using the example of the emotion of pity, which is central to both theater discourse and Rousseau's anthropology:

> Pity is innate, but in its natural purity it is not a peculiarity of man but is quite generally peculiar to living things. [...] Only with the power of imagination does this compassion come to itself in mankind, rise to [...] representation and produce identification with the other as a different ego[59].

And even more succinctly with a view to its pharmacological structure, Derrida states that the imagination "transcends animality and

---

56 J.-J. Rousseau: Collection complète des œuvres, vol. VI, p. 452.
57 Ibid.
58 Ibid., p. 453.
59 J. Derrida: Grammatologie, p. 262.

arouses human compassion only by opening up the scene and the space for theatrical representation. It inaugurates the perversion, the possibility of which is inherent in the very idea of perfection"[60].

Compassion appears here less as a feeling or a virtue, but as a cipher that reveals theatricality as a constitutive basic structure of human intersubjectivity. It is not the theater as an institution and not theatricality as a structural principle of human intersubjectivity that is pathological[61], but the fact that the theater, as Diderot conceives it theoretically and as d'Alembert recommends it to the people of Geneva, fixes one-sided and asymmetrical relationships: between the enlightened playwrights and an audience in need of education, between actors and spectators, between fiction and reality. Due to their passivity, the members of the audience remain dissociated from one another; they are only connected through their one-sided dependence on a common center, the stage and the performance.

With Rousseau, the possibility of a non-alienating theater and a non-pathological theatricality does not remain a merely theoretical possibility. Towards the end of his "Letter to d'Alembert" he hints at two alternatives to a theater *à la parisienne*. First, there is the tradition of popular festivals, anchored in Geneva, in which the asymmetries characteristic of institutionalized theater are eliminated, so that "the chasm between individual and society is temporarily breached"[62]. In Rousseau's words:

> Plant a stake crowned with flowers in the middle of a square; gather the people together there, and you will have a festival. Do better yet; let the spectators become an entertainment to

---

60 Ibid.
61 In this respect, Rousseau's diagnosis bears resemblance to Guy Debord's "The society of the Spectacle". On this see Kohn, Margaret: "Homo spectator. Public space in the age of the spectacle", in: Philosophy & Social Criticism 34 (2008), pp. 467–486, p. 476f.
62 Ibid., p. 472.

themselves; make them actors themselves; do it so that each sees and loves himself in the others so that all will be better united[63].

The second alternative makes use of the form of drama but tries to make the limits of the institution of theater immanently visible in order to destabilize it. Bottici and Kohn refer to a technique elaborated by Guy Debord in the fight against the 'society of the spectacle', diversion or *détournement*: "Détournement means that we cannot get out of the spectacle, but we can use pre-existing elements of it in a new ensemble that subverts, destabilizes, *détourne*, the dominant spectacular logic"[64]. Since Rousseau himself wrote dramas, it would seem particularly appropriate to turn also to them for explication and practical demonstration. Maria Gullstam in her book about theater in Rousseau traces in a nuanced way, "how Rousseau in his plays problematizes the power structures within artistic representation"[65]. She shows that "Rousseau plays with the concepts of both traditional imitation and auto-representation in various ways in order to address the possible harm that theatrical imitation can do, and as a way of encouraging autonomous thinking in the audience"[66].

2.5 The limits of homeopathy in Rousseau

It is appropriate at this point to pull together and systematize our previous individual and example-oriented considerations. Rousseau's diagnosis of contemporary bourgeois society makes use of the disease metaphor, which has a long tradition in political theory. In applying the metaphor, however, he reinterprets the concept of disease. For Rousseau, illness no longer denotes the abandonment of an indisputably presupposed order, a state of temporary disharmony between part and whole (e.g. through the

---

63 J.-J. Rousseau: Collection complète des œuvres, vol. VI, p. 585.
64 C. Bottici: Democracy and the spectacle, p. 242.
65 M. Gullstam: Rousseau's Idea of Theatre, p. 117.
66 Ibid., p. 198.

usurpation of a tyrant who puts himself and his followers above the common interests). Rather, for Rousseau, illness is a structural feature of modern society that systematically produces a series of social pathologies, which manifest themselves in individual suffering due to alienation. In contrast to the classical disease metaphor in politics, which, as an indicator of a disorder was at the same time a pointer to its cure, modern social pathologies cannot simply be addressed through political action. Their underlying mechanisms are complex and difficult to comprehend, as they result from unintended consequences of collective social practices.

Rousseau's original idea is to cure these systemic ills through homeopathic therapy. This form of therapy, the prerequisite of which is a pharmacological analysis of social pathologies, cannot be reduced to clear rules; it is not a form of technology, but of curative practice. This practice cannot be raised to an epistemic level of theory, but its guiding principles can be generalized:

(1) Contextualism: Apt diagnosis, appropriate dosage
According to Rousseau, the most general basis of the homeopathic therapeutic approach is Parcelsus' maxim that it depends solely on the dose whether a substance is a poison or a remedy. "The same causes that have corrupted peoples serve sometimes to prevent even greater corruption. Thus a person who has ruined his temperament by the unwarranted use of medicine must look once more to the physicians to save his life"[67]. The principle applies equally to individual (pedagogical) and collective (political) therapy. In Emile's educational program, everything depends on the student having the right experience at the right time. And in the political shaping of living conditions, the *législateur* must carefully consider the 'age' factor, i.e. the level of cultural development of a people: "For people and nations there is a period of maturation that they must pass through before they can be subjected to laws"[68]. The same applies not only to the establishment of the constitution as a basic political order, but also to the introduction of cultural practices, as Rousseau makes

---

67 Cited after J. Starobinski: The Antidote in the Poison, p. 121.
68 J.-J. Rousseau: Collection complète des œuvres, vol. I, p. 238f.

clear with respect to the above-discussed proposal by d'Alembert to introduce a theater in Geneva. The theater is harmful to peoples in their 'early state', yet "when the people are corrupt, spectacles are good for them."[69]

(2) Therapeutical wisdom as expert knowledge
Given the immense importance of an appropriate diagnosis aimed at the patient, the question arises as to who is able to make such a diagnosis. It appears to be an extremely demanding business; that much is certain. Consequently, Rousseau is skeptical about the possibilities of self-medication. In the case of pedagogical therapy, this seems to be less of a problem, since the pedagogical relationship is structured asymmetrically, but only for the purpose of bringing the student into a symmetrical position in the long term. Nonetheless, Rousseau seems to be skeptical as to whether a capacity for insight on the part of the student is available at an early stage, otherwise the master's lessons could increasingly proceed in the way of argumentative justification instead of strategic control. The success of education, however, seems to be determined primarily by the pharmacological dosage of the right stimuli.

The same pattern can also be seen in the field of political guidance through constitution-making. The profile of qualification that the *législateur* would have to meet is high: it would require a "higher reason that sees all passions of people and has none, that bears no resemblance to our nature, which it knows from top to bottom" — a hardly realistic requirement as Rousseau himself admits: "It would take the gods to give people laws"[70]. Another example of Rousseau's trust in elites is the regulation of cultural innovation. The influence of the arts and sciences on society is so risky that the dosage can only be entrusted to experts — the *Académie* has to act as *gatekeeper* here[71]. Only in his considerations on the writing self does Rousseau come close to admitting the possibility of self-medication.

---

69   Cited after J. Starobinski: The Antidote in the Poison, p. 125.
70   J.-J. Rousseau: Collection complète des œuvres, vol. I, p. 232
71   J. Starobinski: The Antidote in the Poison, p. 121f.

(3) The aim of therapy: Relief vs. Healing
In Rousseau's writings that are critical of culture, especially in the two Discourses, the trend towards decadence does not seem entirely reversible. The therapeutic interventions serve to alleviate the suffering rather than healing in the real sense. In a biographical analysis, Rousseau emphasizes: "As for myself, if I had [...] neither read nor written, I would no doubt have been happier. If letters were now abolished, however, I would be deprived of the only pleasure I have left"[72]. The same figure is found with regard to the effects of the arts and sciences that, "having given birth to many vices, are needed to prevent them from turning into crimes"[73].

In the programmatic writings on educational and political therapy, *Emile* and the *Contrat Social*, the perspective appears more optimistic, and a possible cure comes into focus. Neuhouser consequently gives the chapter in which he analyzes the countermeasures considered by Rousseau the title "Prescriptions"[74]. The point here is to provide individuals with a social infrastructure in both the micro and the macro range that makes successful relationships of recognition possible. In his reconstruction of measures to protect the individual against inflamed *amour propre*, Neuhouser differentiates between approaches in the 'domestic' and in the 'social' sphere. "The remedy of domestic education"[75] encompasses the promotion of self-modesty and a feeling of equality, which is achieved through the responsive handling of children's needs and protection against an early encounter through the comparative 'external gaze'. "Social and political remedies"[76], on the other hand, are intended to guarantee social circumstances that prevent citizens from becoming too dependent on one another, for example by reducing socio-economic inequality and creating "institutional sources of respect and self- esteem"[77], such as political honors.

---

72 Cited after J. Starobinski: The Antidote in the Poison, p. 124.
73 Cited after J. Starobinski: The Antidote in the Poison, p. 121.
74 F. Neuhouser: Rousseau's Theodicy of Self-Love, p. 153ff.
75 Ibid., p. 171ff.
76 Ibid., p. 161ff.
77 Ibid., p. 166.

(4) The limits of homeopathy

The figure of homeopathic healing is used excessively by Rousseau and stretched to the limit of its metaphorical space — at the same time, however, Rousseau leaves no doubt that it is not always possible to make the seeds of good grow. In such cases only the path of a radical new beginning remains open, i.e. revolution:

> Just as some diseases confuse people's minds and rob them of the memory of the past, so there are occasional epochs of violence in the existence of states in which revolutions produce the same effect on peoples as certain crises produce on individuals [...] and the state, set on fire by civil wars, rises, so to speak, from its ashes, escaping the arms of death and regaining the vigor of youth[78].

As Starobinski maintains, in this reflection the remedy is no longer "conceived on the homeopathic model as being *inherent* in the cause of the disease itself", but rather on the "allopathic model as coming from *outside* to combat the disease through administration of a contrary agent"[79].

> In either case the disease will have been useful, but in the former it will have demonstrated its aptitude for transformation from evil into good, whereas in the latter its very severity will have called down the forces of destruction and led to its replacement by an antagonistic power.[80]

Sometimes there is a point of no return that requires a clear cut and a radical new beginning. Nevertheless, this remedy as a last resort is to be used with extreme caution, because here too the basic pharmacological insight implies that the new beginning also contains illness and health from the same source. The revolution, even if it seems inevitable, is, for Rousseau, "almost as much to be feared as the disease it is meant to cure, and which it is blameworthy to desire and impossible to foresee."[81]

---

78 J.-J. Rousseau: Collection complète des œuvres, vol. I, p. 238.
79 J. Starobinski: The Antidote in the Poison, p. 122, our italics.
80 Ibid., p. 122f.
81 Ibid.

Chapter 3: Digital Pharmacology: Stiegler

3.1 Going beyond Rousseau with Rousseau

The reconstruction of Rousseau serves as a useful conceptual framework to interpret Stiegler's conception of pharmacology. On the one hand, some parallels can be found which help to shed light on both Rousseau and Stiegler. On the other hand, against the background of Rousseau's writings we can see more clearly what is specific about a *digital* pharmacology and how Stiegler theoretically goes beyond Rousseau in order to get a view of this current form of techno-cultural evolution.

Four basic similarities stand out: first, there is a certain parallelism in the *basic assumptions* about social development. Both assume a co-evolution of technological, cultural and psychological development. In Rousseau's work, the unstable equilibrium of the state of nature is disturbed by a series of natural disasters, which are necessary for cultural-technological adaptation, and which irreversibly trigger the process of civilization in all its ambivalence.[1] Stiegler conceptualizes this development through the interaction of three levels of organs — technical, social and psychological organs

---

1 Stiegler himself takes Rousseau as a point of departure in his Technics and Time, vol. 1: "Rousseau's narrative of the origin shows us through antithesis how everything of the order of what is usually considered specifically human is immediately and irremediably linked to an absence of property, to a process of 'supplementation', of prosthetisation or exteriorisation, in which nothing is any longer immediately at hand, where everything is instrumentalised, technicised, unbalanced" (p. 133).

— in the development of which the technical organs are something like the pacemaker.[2]

Every development spurt causes a dis-equilibration of the balance of these three organ levels, which is at the same time the germ of both decay and further development — the basic pharmacological figure. While further development means that the new technical organs are appropriated on the psychological level and embedded on the social level (*adoption*), there is a risk of decay if the psychological and social organ levels merely adapt reactively to technological changes (*adaptation*). Thus for Stiegler, technologies are never ever inherently pathological or harmful, but always only the forms of life in which they are embedded. In view of the profusion of digital technologies that is characteristic of the present, however, it seems as if it were becoming more and more difficult to adopt technology in a productive and appropriate way. In a nutshell, the problem for Bernard Stiegler is that technical inventions which operate at "lightning speed"[3] — a phrase he uses repeatedly — outpace cultural adaptation[4]. It seems as if people can do nothing but react to an ever-increasing stream of technical innovations.

A second parallel exists in terms of the *consequences* that this disequilibrating brings about in the respective contemporary societies. Both Rousseau and Stiegler belong to the camp of cultural critics who decipher the epoch-typical suffering of people as social pathologies. The phenomenon of *divertissement*, of confusion caused by an overwhelming amount of input, of a huge variety of stimuli, seems to be a common ground. What vanity is to Rousseau, attention disorders and various forms of addiction are to Stiegler. He characterizes our society as an "addictogenic society", where the "drive-based tendencies are systematically exploited while its subli-

---

2   For a detailed reconstruction, see Abbinnett, Ross: The Thought of Bernard Stiegler. Capitalism, Technology and the Politics of Spirit, London: Routledge 2017, pp. 37–63.

3   Stiegler, Bernard: The Age of Disruption. Technology and Madness in Computational Capitalism, Cambridge et al: Polity Press 2019, p. 7.

4   B. Stiegler: Technics and Time, p. 15.

matory tendencies are systematically short-circuited"[5]. For Stiegler, these processes culminate in a loss of "attention", which is not only visible in the literal attention disorders as an individual psychological problem, but also in a loss of civility in social relationships. Attention, i.e. the ability to focus intellectual faculties and to relate them to non-existent objects, counterfactuals, ideas, values, is for Stiegler the central human faculty that enables a productive use of technology as opposed to a merely reactive one.[6]

If social pathology is the object of criticism, a state of health must be conceivable as a normative corrective. This is the case with Stiegler. In line with Rousseau, who does not understand the normal and the pathological as opposites, Stiegler defines health as the creative handling of toxic dispositives:

> When experiencing the pathological, life is normative: it invents states of health [...]. Health is characterized by the ability to transcend the norm that defines what is currently normal, the ability to tolerate violations of the usual norm and to introduce new norms in new situations.[7]

Here a third fundamental parallel to Rousseau becomes clear with regard to the characterization of the endangered intellectual capabilities, the *proprium humanum*. For Rousseau social progress threatens the authenticity of the person and their will, i.e. ultimately their ability to desire. Inauthentic forms of sociality and social comparison as the basis for the definition of what is individually desirable lead to the development of false passions based on an unleashed imagination. Stiegler's criticism aims in a related direction. In a slightly different terminological diction informed by psychoanaly-

---

5   Stiegler, Bernard: What Makes Life Worth Living. On Pharmacology, Cambridge et al.: Polity Press 2013, p. 27.
6   See in particular: B. Stiegler: What Makes Life Worth Living, p. 82.
7   Stiegler, Bernard: "Licht und Schatten im digitalen Zeitalter", in: Ramón Reichert (Ed.), Big Data. Analysen zum digitalen Wandel von Wissen, Macht, Ökonomie, Bielefeld: transcript 2014, pp. 35–46, p. 43.

sis he employs the conception of a "libidinal economy of desire"[8]. For him the ability to pay attention is also part of the ability to desire: it creates desires and enables their sublimation — an ability that is almost completely regressed in addictive behavior.[9] The conceptual framework of general organology[10] allows Stiegler to place "desire" and the technical environment in a fundamental relationship of co-constitution: desire is created by "tools" with which one constructs a future for oneself[11]: the plasticity of the drive structure is formed depending on the available tools that enable satisfaction in the near or distant future. Technologies that systematically guarantee short-term satisfaction, as many digital devices do, outsource this to the technical organ: the result is "exteriorization without return — that is, without re-interiorization"[12].

Fourth, both Rousseau and Stiegler alternate between homeopathic and allopathic remedies when they outline *possible solutions* to the pharmacological question. We will describe this difference in more detail later; however, it seems helpful to note that both Rousseau and Stiegler think that the remedy for intoxication could be based on applying either a more skillful dosage or different *pharmaka*. This would, of course, imply that the "loneliness" of the *"promeneur solitaire"* in his last writings could also be read as a *pharmakon*.

---

8   B. Stiegler: What Makes Life Worth Living, p. 24f.; see also Stiegler, Bernard: "Pharmacology of Desire: Drive-based capitalism and libidinal dis-economy", in: New Formations 72 (2011), pp. 150–161.

9   "The formation of desire is characterized by addiction when adhesive libido attaches itself to pharmaka that generate rhythms and expectations of such immediate reward that the focus of attention becomes narrowly fixated on the present." (B. Stiegler: What Makes Life Worth Living: p. 25,).

10 Stiegler, Bernard: "Elements for a General Organology", in: Derrida Today 13 (2020), pp. 72–94, DOI: 10.3366/drt.2020.0220.

11 B. Stiegler: What Makes Life Worth Living, p. 24–25.

12 Stiegler, Bernard: "Die Aufklärung in the Age of Philosophical Engineering", Computational Culture 2 (2012b), http://computationalculture.net/die-auf klarung-in-the-age-of-philosophical-engineering/ (01.02.2021), p. 10.

While in the four points mentioned Stiegler's pharmacology can be understood as an update and further development of Rousseau's conception, in two regards he goes well beyond Rousseau. On the one hand, he poses the question of responsibility and asks what kinds of social and political actors benefit from the processes he describes as harmful to society. In the case of Rousseau, "society" seems to be an amorphous agent of alienation; Stiegler names the business-models which monetarize the destruction of human attention. He explicitly criticizes the coalition of the actors of financial market capitalism with the entertainment industries, a form of "globalized psycho-power [which] is the systematic organization of the capture of attention made possible by the psycho-technologies that have developed with radio (1920), television (1950) and digital technologies (1990)"[13].

The fact that he understands the grievances as the outcome of exploitation is evident in his replacement of the concept of alienation, which was central to Rousseau, by the term "proletarianization", which he adopts from Marx, but which he removes from its social-historical context and generally defines as the loss of knowledge through the delegation of activities to an artificial organ. The proletarianization of the producer, criticized by Marx as a paradigmatic relationship of exploitation of the industrial workers, is only the first stage of an overarching cultural rationalization process, which Stiegler describes as "a process of generalized proletarianization"[14]. The first stage of the "proletarianization of the producer", in which only the skill (*savoir-faire*) is outsourced to machines, is followed by two further stages, the proletarianization of the consumer by the entertainment industry, which leads to an outsourcing of *savoir-vivre* and, finally, the delegation of thinking and making decisions (*noesis*) to machines in the present through digital smart technologies.

On the other hand, Stiegler can concretize how the technological media change is altering psychological structures by breaking new

---

13 B. Stiegler: What Makes Life Worth Living, p. 81.
14 B. Stiegler: What Makes Life Worth Living, p. 27.

ground with the concept of "grammatization", which raises pharmacological analysis to a new level. The concept stems from the discourse on grammatology and Derrida's theory on the structuring power of written language,[15] but is expanded by Stiegler in the context of his general organology to an encompassing theory that explains how technological changes reconfigure social and psychological systems: "I have myself extended this concept", Stiegler writes, "by arguing that grammatisation (*sic*) more generally describes all technical processes that enable behavioral fluxes or flows to be made discrete [...] and to be reproduced, those behavioral flows through which are expressed or imprinted the experiences of human beings (speaking, working, perceiving, interacting and so on). If grammatisation is understood in this way, then the digital is the most recent stage of grammatisation."[16] Grammatization thus encompasses all "processes by which a material, sensory, or symbolic flux becomes a gramme"[17] — "gramme" being the Greek term for "written mark".

Elements of grammatization are a *formalization* of hitherto opaque processes by a "spatialization of time" through "materialization"[18]; this results in the *reproducibility* of these processes which thus become objects of control and criticism, hence bringing about reflexivity.[19]

By moving away from the paradigm of writing, Stiegler can comprehend central technological innovation processes such as

---

15 On Derrida and Stiegler, see R. Abbinnett: The Thought of Bernard Stiegler, ch. 1, p. 11ff; see also Ross, Daniel: "Pharmacology and Critique after Deconstruction", in: Christina Howells/Gerald Moore (Eds.), Stiegler and Technics, Edinburgh: Edinburgh University Press 2013, pp. 243–258.

16 B. Stiegler: Die Aufklärung in the Age of Philosophical Engineering, p. 5 (English source text in British spelling).

17 Tinnell, John: "Grammatization: Bernard Stiegler's Theory of Writing and Technology", in: Computers and Composition 37 (2015), pp. 132–146, p. 135.

18 B. Stiegler: Die Aufklärung in the Age of Philosophical Engineering, p. 5f.

19 Stiegler, Bernard: "The Most Precious Good in the Era of Social Technologies", in: Geert Lovink/Miriam Rasch (Eds.), Unlike Us Reader. Social Media Monopolies and their Alternatives, Amsterdam: Institute of Network Cultures 2013b, pp. 16–30, p. 25.

the invention of typeface and letterpress printing, but also industrialization, the bio- and nanotechnological revolution[20] and digitalization as stages in grammatization. In contrast to both a deterministic and a constructivist understanding of human-techno-relations, Stiegler's perspective allows one to conceive of them as co-constituted through grammatization[21].

Stiegler's conception of grammatization, together with his critical focus on the economic and political structures in which changes in the technical infrastructure are embedded, provides him with a powerful analytical tool to scrutinize processes of digitalization which are currently unfolding. Three aspects will be reconstructed here in some detail: the grammatization of the "reading brain", the grammatization of social relations and the grammatization of image consciousness.

3.2 Digital Grammatization I or: from the 'reading brain' to the 'twitter brain'

The paradigmatic example of a grammatization process is the series of innovations set in motion by the invention of written language. Stiegler basically distinguishes between two epochs in this overarching process: the introduction of alphabetical writing in ancient Greece, which "opened up the possibility of the *politeia*, of positive law and of isonomy"[22]. And the spread of the written language through the development of the printing press and the associated literacy, first of the bourgeoisie and then of ever wider sections of the population, which led to the Reformation, Counter-Reformation and the Enlightenment, opening a critical space for a reading audience.

---

20   B. Stiegler: What Makes Life Worth Living, pp. 116f., 129f.
21   Ibid., p. 134.
22   Stiegler, Bernard: "The Carnival of the New Screen: From Hegemony to Isonomy", in: Pelle Snickars/Patrick Vonderau (Eds.), The YouTube reader, Stockholm: National Library of Sweden 2010, pp. 40–59, p. 45.

In order to describe in some detail how the psychological organ level underwent a profound change in the course of this process, he refers to the text "Writing the Self", in which Foucault introduces writing as a technique of the self, as it was already analyzed by Rousseau as a medium of auto-pharmacological control. However, he does not stop here, but underpins these rather hermeneutic interpretations by hard facts that give empirical evidence to the idea of a "re-writing" of the self.[23] Stiegler takes up Maryanne Wolf's concept of a "reading brain" — a prerequisite, as it were, for the "writing self". Wolf's neuroscientific research has shown that reading changes the neuroplasticity of the brain and enables abstract thinking operations that were previously inaccessible: "In much the way reading reflects the brain's capacity for going beyond the original design of its structures, it also reflects the reader's capacity to go beyond what is given by the text and the author"[24].

With a view to the human faculty of attention, which is central to Stiegler, reading trains a skill that Stiegler describes as "deep attention", based on Patricia Hayles' definition of the term. Hayles describes deep attention as "a precious social achievement that took centuries, even millennia, to cultivate, facilitated by the spread of libraries, better K-12 schools, more access to colleges and universities, and so forth. Indeed, certain complex tasks can be accomplished only with deep attention: it is a heritage we cannot afford to lose"[25].

It is precisely the loss of this capacity for deep attention that Hayles fears in the age of digital reading. Key factors here are the serial consumption of digital snippets of text via Twitter, the distraction from the text content on websites through constant cross-references in the form of colored hyperlinks, the impossibility of portioning a screen text in the form of discrete pages and connecting it with haptic impressions. All of this, according to Hayles, promotes a different, less focused form of attention, which she refers

---

23 B. Stiegler: Elements for a General Organology, p. 81ff.
24 M. Wolf: Proust and the Squid, p. 15.
25 Hayles, N. Katherine: How We Think. Digital Media and Contemporary Technogenesis, Chicago, IL: University of Chicago Press 2012, p. 99.

to as "hyper-attention". More figuratively, but in much in the same vein, Wolf speaks of "twitter brains" that the digital reader is likely to develop.[26] Despite their respective critical perspectives, Hayles and Wolf are far from seeing hyper-attention as an inferior or privative cognitive mode. In Hayles' view, both modes have advantages and disadvantages. "Deep attention is superb for solving complex problems represented in a single medium, but it comes at the price of environmental alertness and flexibility of response. Hyper-attention excels at negotiating rapidly changing environments in which multiple foci compete for attention"[27].

However, she delivers a clear warning of the danger that deep attention, which is already less developed in the younger generation, could eventually be completely lost — a problem that she sees as a challenge for pedagogy and the educational system. Wolf also subscribes to this view, recommending that children have no contact with digital screens up to age two, and only limited and supervised access later on, in order to leave room for analogous "slow" reading.[28]

In the terminology developed by Starobinski, these recommendations seem to suggest an *allopathic* treatment of the pharmacology of digital reading that maintains a reserve of paper-based reading in an otherwise digitalized world.

As much as Stiegler draws on the analyses of Wolf and Hayles regarding the transformation of the cognitive organ level in a digital environment, he distances himself clearly from their pragmatic solution proposals. In his view, pharmacological analysis must take on a political dimension, and in two ways: first, it is a matter of naming who is responsible for and who will benefit from the changes. This is because, in his opinion, the destruction of deep attention is not

---

26 Cited after an interview with Maryanne Wolf by Haas, Michaela: "Wir bekommen Twitter Gehirne", NZZ-online, 27.3.2019 https://www.nzz.ch/folio/wir-bekommen-twitter-gehirne-ld.1622968 (10.9.2021).

27 Hayles, N. Katherine: "Hyper and Deep Attention: The Generational Divide in Cognitive Modes", Profession (2007), pp. 187–199, p. 188.

28 Wolf, Maryanne: Reader, Come Home. The Reading Brain in a Digital World, New York/London/Toronto/Sydney: Harper, 2019.

an unforeseen side-effect of digitalization. Rather, the audiovisual (i.e. film and television) and programming industries are systematically targeting its erosion out of commercial interest. And secondly, the cognitive changes always also affect the organization of social coexistence — the psychological and social organ levels are interdependent: according to Stiegler, deep attention is coupled with "the lengths of the circuits of transindividuation [...] Each circuit (and its length) consists of many connections that also form a network, as another constituent of depth, a kind of texture"[29].

Against this backdrop it becomes clear that the question of the digital transformation of the mind cannot be regarded independently of the question of the digital reconfiguration of social relations.

3.3 Digital Grammatization II or: friendship in the 'digital anthill'

How fruitful Stiegler's broad concept of grammatization is for the interpretation of the psycho-social reconfiguration in the digital world can be illustrated by his pharmacological analysis of friendship networks in social media: "[S]ocial networks represent a stage within a process of grammatization, which leads to the grammatization of social relations as such"[30], Stiegler claims. The grammatization of friendship, the most prominent example of which is Facebook, comprises the three levels of grammatization differentiated above, i.e. formalization, discretization and reflectivity. First, friendship is formalized on social networks because it can only be concluded after a request and its confirmation by the addressee. It thus becomes the product of an act of mutual explicit consent. At the same time, the implicit logic of friendly connections is made explicit through social networks and made the subject of algorithmic computing processes that search for common ground

---

29   Stiegler, Bernard: Taking Care of Youth and the Generations, Transl. Stephen Barker, Stanford, CA: Stanford University Press 2010, p. 80.

30   B. Stiegler: The Most Precious Good in the Era of Social Technologies, p. 25.

among the users and make suggestions for obvious connections. The pharmacological question is whether these transformations lead to an increase in reflectivity, thus opening up a space for a genuine adoption of friendship in the digital era, or in Stiegler's words: whether "in digital, also known as social, networks [they amount to] a *philia* regressing us to the state of insects", or whether "they constitute a novel opportunity to achieve this elusive *philotès* among humans"[31].

Much more than in the field of digital reading, Stiegler sees the potential of a positive pharmacology here: The rules of algorithmic selection and the revelation of the "gramme" of social relationships need not lead to an erosion of the idea of friendship, but could also bring about a new reflective quality in social relationships. For Stiegler, the self-profiling and self-indexing required of Facebook users have the potential to foster "auto-ethnography" and "auto-sociography", which can result in an explication of the social rules of relationality on which the 'real' network of social relationships is based. This level of social rules which establish the logic of the formation of friendships, but also the constitution of the individual participant, is what Stiegler calls "transindividuation". Processes of grammatization make these rules reflexive.

As a historical example, Stiegler cites the establishment of a legal understanding of citizenship in Greek antiquity, which was nothing other than the expression of the social reality of the polis as coexistence in formalized friendship:

> [C]itizenship forming is grounded on the descriptive grammatization of social relationships by way of the written script in the service of an intensification of the psychical individuation of each citizen, and through him or her, of the other citizens, leading by progressive extension, to collective individuation[32].

Against this background, Stiegler also sees opportunities for further grammatization of social relationships through social networks: "I do believe that the reflexivity included in the public declaration of

---

31   Ibid., p. 20
32   Ibid., p. 24

relationships (friendly and otherwise) could lead [...] to the emergence of a process of psychical, collective and technical individuation, which would indeed make for a relationally peaceful or benevolent 21st century, grounded in — if I dare to say — a new benevolence"[33].

What stands in the way of this positive outlook, however, is the data capitalist organization of social networks. Stiegler brands the machine matching of profiles as a form of "surgical marketing"[34], through which friendship loses the status of a relationship that is not subject to utility calculation and falls victim to economic exploitation. The selection rules of digital script mechanisms are anything but transparent: in fact, they disguise themselves so that the networker remains a mere user (subject to rules given by others). In order to unleash the positive potential of the digital in social networking, it would be necessary, according to Stiegler, "[to] reverse the pharmacologic direction of social networks" and "make these networks capable of becoming agents of reflexivity"[35]. Two changes would be required for this. On a technical level, more transparency would have to be created, with the selection rules being determined and designed by the users themselves, as in open-source software programing. But there is a second, social level that comes into play in diagnosing the structure of needs that makes the groundbreaking success of social networks such as Facebook explicable. Digital networks function for the younger generation as "a 'cure' for the lack of social relations, just as games are a relief for the social desert in which young adults live"[36]. This need is intended to be met by linking digital networks back to established social forms: "I believe that the real issue is about the arrangement of social networks with social groups (since a social network without a social group is equivalent

---

[33] Ibid., p. 22.
[34] Ibid.
[35] Ibid., p. 26.
[36] Ibid., p. 28.

to a mafia)"³⁷: "we need to create policed, meaning politicized communities of friends in the social networks"³⁸.

3.4 Digital Grammatization III or: the alphabetization of image consciousness

The change in the cognitive apparatus and culture through alphabetic writing is a paradigmatic case of a grammatization process, but only one case in the larger history of the co-evolution of technology and humanity. Digitalization leads to a discretization of other domains like the *visible*, and this in turn opens up the possibility of developing a new visual literacy enabling the observer to critically analyze images and break them down in order to create new ones from their discrete elements — to 'read' and '(re-)write' images, as it were.³⁹ In his lecture "The Discrete Image" Stiegler argues that the digitalization of the image, which is resolved by a technical process into a finite number of discrete elements (pixels), in a way yields an 'alphabet' of the visible world, which makes new forms of image perception and image construction possible.

Stiegler's argument is based on the opposition of analog and digital photography, whereby — following Roland Barthes — he ascribes an aura of authenticity to the analog photo, which is evident in the belief "this was ..."⁴⁰. The analog photo nourishes the viewer's already existing tendency towards everyday Platonism⁴¹. However, moments of discretization are already inherent in analog photography, because in the frame of the photo a specific perspec-

---

37 Ibid.
38 Ibid., p. 29.
39 Stiegler, Bernard: "The Discrete Image", in: Derrida, Jacques/Stiegler, Bernard (Eds.), Echographies of television. Filmed Interviews, Cambridge: Polity Press 2002, pp. 145–163, p. 162f.
40 Ibid., p. 158.
41 Sontag, Susan: On Photography, New York: Delta Books 1977, pp. 3–24 (chapter entitled "In Plato's Cave").

tive becomes visible[42], which manifests a difference between "image-object" and "mental-image"[43]. This difference is reinforced by the digitalization of photography, because the constructional character of the picture is now made explicit on a technical level and — so Stiegler's hope — is anchored not only on the level of image production, but also on the level of image reception.

Just as reading and writing, i.e. the reception and production of written language, tend to go hand-in-hand, so, according to Stiegler, the alphabetization of the visual domain also offers the opportunity to reduce the structural gap between image producers and image consumers, which is a characteristic of the radio and television program industry.[44] The grammatization of the visual accelerated in the 1980s with technical innovations such as portable camcorders and home video systems. These technologies, which put the generation and processing of moving images in the hands of amateurs, made the discretization of image streams possible for the first time through functions such as freezing the image, slow motion, rewinding etc. According to Stiegler, all these "deeply modify relations to the audiovisual temporal flux, allowing one to imagine the appearance of a more reflective and less consumerist gaze"[45].

Stiegler has spelled out this potential for liberation, especially with a view to moving images (which are even more formative

---

42 B. Stiegler: The Discrete Image, p. 155.

43 Ibid., p. 162.

44 The idea of empowering people who have been degraded to consumers through traditional media to self-determined "prosumers" is one of the oldest hopes associated with digitalization. In view of the psycho-technological advancement of digital marketing through innovations aimed at the subtle influencing of users' psychological processes instigated and controlled by big data analytics, such as "micro-targeting" and "affective computing", these early hopes, however, have been dampened. On this see Bösel, Bernd: "Der psychotechnologische Komplex — Die Automatisierung mentaler Prozesse als demokratietheoretisches Problem", in: Zeitschrift für Politikwissenschaft (2021), https://doi.org/10.1007/s41358-021-00283-2.

45 B. Stiegler: The Carnival of the New Screen, p. 41.

than photographs for our imagination and memories), using the YouTube platform as an example. The positive opportunity associated with a provider like YouTube is that it "breaks, precisely, with the opposition between consumption and production, and therefore constitutes the possibility of implementing a new distributed and decentralized network of renewable energy in which everyone could be both producer and consumer"[46].

Similar to the grammatization of social relationships in digital social networks, Stiegler sees a potential for reconfiguring the rules of transindividuation here. On the psychological organ level he hopes for the "production of a new kind of deep attention"[47], while on the social organ level he expects that the "combination of auto-broadcasting, auto-production and auto-indexation can create processes of transindividuation that short-circuit the short circuits engendered by the top-down system of the cultural industries through a bottom-up movement"[48].

In his 2002 lecture on the "discrete image", Stiegler takes a rather techno-deterministic view that appears optimistic with regard to the development of the emancipatory potential.[49] Later, however, he insisted that the liberation could only be the result of a "political battle"[50] which would lead to a replacement of our careless way of dealing with the collective grammatization by collective care: "The therapeutic question is then to know how the discretization can be curative — i.e. constituting an isonomy supporting autonomy — and what the political, cultural and industrial conditions of such care are."[51] We would like to propose the term *cura publica* for this collective curative attitude, in order to emphasize its political

---

46 B. Stiegler, What Makes Life Worth Living, p. 93.
47 B. Stiegler: The Carnival of the New Screen, p. 56.
48 Ibid., p. 55.
49 Nathan diagnoses an "overweening optimism about digital technology", see Nathan, Usha Manaithunai: On the Possibility of Visual Literacy and New Intentions with Digital Images, National University of Singapore 2011, https://core.ac.uk/download/pdf/48646006.pdf (01.02.2022), p. 10.
50 B. Stiegler: The Carnival of the New Screen, p. 47.
51 Ibid., p. 48.

dimension: there are not only *Public Things*, but there is also, if things go well, a *cura publica*.

Chapter 4: Exploring the Limits of Pharmacology

4.1 Homeopathic, allopathic, and heteropathic pharmacology

If we take a step back, the question arises as to whether the idea of 'pharmacological analysis' is not only suitable for a systematization of "what is going on", but whether it might even constitute a type of theory which allows a form of social criticism — even beyond Rousseau's critique of contemporary bourgeois society. We have already seen that the distinction between different ways of practicing self-medication or auto-pharmacology is of great importance. We would now like to take a closer look at three ideal-types of pharmacological practice.

Re-reading Rousseau's texts as documents of an auto-pharmacological quest allows one to extract some important distinctions. First of all, what looked like "autonomy" can now be conceptualized as successful auto-pharmacology. Not the *nómos*, the rule or law, is at the heart of the matter, but the *pharmakon*. *Nomoi* are *pharmaka* in the sense that they allow a self-determination and self-evaluation. But not all *pharmaka* are *nomoi*: theatre, reading, and writing are the most important *pharmaka* that Rousseau discusses. Their use is homeo-pathic in that they try to heal what their misuse has caused.

This re-reading of Rousseau also allows us to distinguish more clearly between three variations of pharmacology: *homeopathic, allopathic* and *heteropathic*. The last, the *heteropathic*, is by far the most interesting approach, as it takes an orthogonal position: it fights fire neither with fire nor with water, but sidesteps the problem by proposing a different (*heteron*) *pharmakon*. This approach seems particularly suitable for digital pharmacology, because it offers escape from the opposition between two polar choices: either a digital "cold turkey", or the surrender to digital *pharmaka* that takes place when apps are used in order to gain control over one's excessive smartphone use.

Let's illustrate how *heteropathic auto-pharmacology* works. In the movie *T2 Trainspotting* (Danny Boyle, 2017) two ex-junkies look back on their youth, which was at the center of the first *Transpotting* movie of 1993. Two of the main characters, Mark and Spud, go for a run and finally end up on a hill, looking down on the city of Edinburgh. Mark explains his heteropathic approach. Detox has never worked, and his advice to Spud is: "Be addicted to something else!" The two friends discuss different options: running, boxing, writing etc.

In the context of *Trainspotting* this advice has a specific connotation: trainspotting as a pastime is not only about drug consumption, but also about social stratification. All the drug-users among Mark's friends are from the working-class; his ex-girlfriend, however, clearly belongs to the upper-middle-class. She ends up as a lawyer and looks down on Mark and his friends. Apparently, their social class had no other *pharmaka* to offer that would have helped Mark and his friends avoid heroin. The most sinister and depressing scenes of the film show Mark's parents watching TV-shows.

A possible hypothesis might therefore be that a plurality of *pharmaka* is the privilege of particular social classes, and to counterbalance *pharmaka* with other *pharmaka* is possible if (and only if!) a variety of *pharmaka* is available. The British upper-class in the 19th century had sports, music, champagne, fox-hunting, religion, cigars, literature and whiskey; the working class had beer and gin. Thus the plurality of *pharmaka* accessible to one, we could conclude, indicates one's social status.

This perspective would frame mono-pharmacology as potentially problematic: to use only or predominantly *one pharmakon* might be a dangerous practice, because it tends to lead to overdosing. Religious fanatism would then look like a dubious monopharmacological practice in which being abstinent from other *pharmaka* triggers an overuse of religion (and vice-versa). It seems to be more than a coincidence that fanatic Islamists and jihadists often refuse other *pharmaka*, just as the fundamentalist Christians in the Bible-belt tend towards abstinence. All the emotional management and self-regulation then needs to be done by religion — overburdening both religion and the subject which is using it. Poly-pharmacological use may thus prevent psychological mayhem.

There seems to be a structural analogy between this view and Nietzsches's criticism of monotheism. In his view, the polytheism of the Greeks was the more human, more life-oriented and colorful way of looking at the world. The Greeks were not only polytheists, but also poly-pharmacologists. They had a very elaborate culture of provoking different kinds of ecstasy, and a complex system of transgenerational education concerning the skills needed for life. In Nietzsche's view, both Judaism and Christianity lacked this Greek serenity; they already suffered from what we could now redescribe as mono-pharmacology.

Obviously we should be careful about taking Nietzsche's view at face-value. After all, both Judaism and Christianity developed complex systems of poly-pharmacology. What is more inspiring is Nietzsche's view on the social stratification linked to this question: when Nietzsche describes both Judaism and Christianity as religions of slaves, he is pointing to the glorification of weakness, in particular in Christianity. However, we could also ask the question as to what degree social stratification is linked to a certain pharmacological polyphonic capability.

This would explain why heteropathic approaches in pharmacology are so difficult. In *T2 Trainspotting* the character of Spud has to develop the capability to use writing as a *pharmakon* which allows him to stay away from heroin. To find "something else" to be "addicted" to presupposes specific skills.

Rousseau's quest for autonomy now can be re-conceptualized differently. With Rousseau the paradigm of digital pharmacology shares the idea of human plasticity: living a human life is not to "create" oneself, but to define and re-define oneself by habits, decisions, and *pharmaka*. This process of constant "autonomy" now redefined as auto-pharmacology has its limits, of course. However, alongside allopathic and homeopathic approaches the heteropathic approach of sidestepping destructive *pharmaka*-use by taking up other *pharmaka* offers promising solutions in many cases.

The most important lesson we can learn from Rousseau might be, however, that auto-pharmacology fails when it is understood as a solipsistic project: the Rousseau of the *promeneur solitaire* may be happy, but he is in an unstable, endangered state of mind. His happiness always risks shifting towards madness and desperation. In a way, solitude has become his only *pharmakon* and therefore all the problems of mono-pharmacology are present.

Hegel's way of transposing Rousseau's idea of autonomy to the level of the state seems to provide a more compelling answer to the challenge of auto-pharmacology: in order to learn, you have to learn *from someone*. Institutions ensure that the transposition of knowledge from one generation to the other is achieved. A community of auto-pharmacologists is always already a learning community.

4.2 How to do political pharmacology: 'liberal' or 'republican'

The whole point of the term *pharmacology* consists in the fact that it allows one to compare different pharmacological regimes, traditions, and governmentalities. Every culture in every epoch appears to have created its own pharmacological grammar: societies define what is acceptable and what isn't, what is prestigious and what isn't. And these explicit and implicit definitions have a huge impact on the *pharmaka* that are produced and distributed. The shift from alcohol use to caffeine use in Europe in the 18th century, for instance, had an enormous impact on the cultural and political landscape. Whereas alcohol had dominated the pharmacological field for centuries and served as a way of preventing the transmission of diseases via drinking water, caffeine had a different impact. Some scholars have argued that the rise of democracy starting in the 18th century can partly be explained by the rise of coffee-houses where caffeine-animated debate took place.¹ Today, caffeine-consumption is a widespread element of a competitive global economy which demands that everyone be constantly alert.

In order to gain some orientation in the complex field of political pharmacology (and pharma-policy), it is helpful to distinguish two ideal-types in the regulation of a modern society. On the one hand, the liberal approach emphasizes individual freedom and individual responsibility. The liberal tradition argues that the market should allow grown up citizens to make their own decisions. State-intervention is usually viewed as a kind of paternalism, a typical way of framing state-regulation is the concept of the "Nanny-State". Legalizing cannabis, for example, is therefore considered to be a liberal idea, as it puts the responsibility for appropriate use of a substance into the hands of the individual. The mechanism of the market in this paradigm becomes a crucial element, for it is the market which decides on the options of the individual.

The contrasting political tradition could be summarized as "republican": this emphasizes the *res publica*, the perspective of public affairs, the common good, and *shared* responsibility. The concept of freedom from a republican point of view should not be restricted to "negative freedom",² i.e. freedom *from* state-intervention, but should also include the possibility to participating in collectively binding decisions. Input-legitimacy is what makes republican politics democratic, not the restriction of state-intervention. Citizens are therefore viewed not as an unbound self, as a *homo oeconomicus*, but as a *citoyen*, i.e. as citizens engaging with their political community.

This schematic distinction could be refined by adducing a wealth of historical detail on the interaction between liberal and republican traditions in political thought. The main point, however, is the following: the organization of social interaction will always have to

---

1 Schivelbusch, Wolfgang: Tastes of Paradise. A Social History of Spices, Stimulants, and Intoxicants, New York: Vintage Books 1993.

2 Instead of summarizing this debate in detail, we will simply name the most important proponents of contemporary Republicanism: Michael Sandel, Philippe Pettit, Quentin Skinner.

locate itself somewhere on the spectrum of privatization on the one hand and collectivism on the other hand. A democratic state will always have to decide whether things need to be regulated or if they can be left to the free-floating forces of the market. Both options imply very different and specific grammars framing the democratic process. Our proposition is to use this distinction in order to extrapolate two kinds of pharmacology: liberal and republican. The way we use *pharmaka* can be viewed as a private enterprise, providing private joy, private advantages, but also private risk. It can also be viewed as a common task, a collective challenge which needs to be discussed and regulated by collectively binding decisions. As we are currently exploring the possibilities and difficulties of a digital pharmacology, the distinction might help us to evaluate the options.

The distinction between a republican and a liberal approach in pharmacology is related to different ways of organizing public health in general. Public health can be viewed primarily either as a result of individual efforts — or as common challenge. The different reactions to the Covid-crisis in 2020 and 2021 illustrate the enormous ramifications of this difference. A liberal approach would emphasize the individual responsibility to protect oneself; wearing a mask then primarily aims at protecting oneself. From a republican point of view, public health is a common good that can only be achieved by a coordinated effort, by collectively binding decisions and rules that are applied to everyone.

4.3 The toolbox of digital pharmacology

Analogies, we have argued, can serve to explore new territory: what they suggest needs to be tested, elaborated, reconsidered. What would we see if we pushed the idea of digital pharmacology to its limits? The analogy of "classical", i.e. chemical pharmacology and digital pharmacology provides us with a huge set of political mechanisms which seem to have helped dealing with non-digital *pharmaka*:

a) The political ontology of substances
Stiegler himself claimed that an ontology of *pharmaka* in the strict sense wasn't possible. Indeed, the "pharmakon-in-itself" ("an-sich", as Kant would say) seems impossible to extract from the levels of framing, contexts and usages. However, there is an ontology of *pharmaka* as a social practice: societies define classes of substances and they categorize different kinds of *pharmaka*. We distinguish stimulants, sedatives, painkillers etc. It is important to remember that these social constructions have very real consequences. The social ontology of *pharmaka* defines whether a product is put on the free market or whether its access is restricted. The classes of substances are usually rather elaborate in their definition: there are substances you are allowed to buy in a supermarket, others are only sold in a pharmacy and of these many require a prescription. And then there are substances such as strong, addictive painkillers which are administered only by medical authorities under medical supervision and are not allowed at all to be placed in the hands of patients. In the case of digital *pharmaka* we are only just beginning to develop useful categories. Distinguishing different techniques, algorithms, exploits or addictive mechanisms would be a preliminary requirement for dealing with them properly, and developing the art of using them in a skillful way. The analogy would therefore imply the option of establishing well-defined categories and classes of digital *pharmaka*. Is this a task we should carry out collectively? A republican digital pharmacology would imply a public categorization and a public definition of different digital *pharmaka*.

b) Exploring the effects of specific pharmaka
In all Western societies the research on *pharmaka* seems to be both a public and a private good. On the one hand the pharmaceutical industry uses private investment to develop new drugs. On the other hand, there is a public interest in supervising this process. Not only does every democracy have some kind of a "Food and Drug Administration", the famous FDA. Most democracies also provide public infrastructures which allow the study of *pharmaka* outside an economic framework. Universities, for instance, provide the opportunity to study the effects of drugs, substances and behavioral pat-

terns. What would be the analogy in digital pharmacology? At the moment almost all research on digital pharmacology is done in the private sector: Google, Facebook, Netflix, Youtube etc. It's the big players who develop new *pharmaka* and analyze their effects. This research is usually directly linked to marketing-models and is driven by the interest of selling advertising or products and gaining data or money. Only in rare cases do public universities produce elaborated research on digital pharmacology. As far as the exploration of digital *pharmaka* is concerned, we are operating in an extremely liberal framework. However, analyzing digital rhetoric, exploits, micro-targeting etc. could however also be viewed as a public task.

c) Regulating consumption
The regulation of non-digital *pharmaka* is a huge field in which very different tools and mechanisms are used. The consumption of chemical *pharmaka* can be influenced by mandatory instruction leaflets: consumers need to be informed about what they use. The equivalent can be found in the "terms and conditions" that we usually quickly agree on when we want to use an online service. A sharper method of influencing the use of *pharmaka* are taxes. The Scandinavian countries are known for taxing alcohol in a rather extreme way; in Sweden or Norway a small bottle of beer can easily be priced at an equivalent of 10 USD. Regulating the use of digital *pharmaka* could also be tried by taxing exploits or cookies.

A specific challenge would be to consider interaction between non-digital and digital *pharmaka*; although it seems difficult to prevent such interaction, the massive mixed consumption of caffeine, alcohol and news is a global phenomenon which requires systematic research. Mixed consumption is, of course, not at all a new practice; it is reflected in classical habits such as reading the newspaper and drinking a cup of coffee in the morning, which can now be framed differently: as a double triggering of dopamine via caffeine and pleasurable mental stimulation at the same time.

d) Protecting the population; i.e. pharmacological "bio-politics"
A classic example of a pre-digital biopolitical attempt to regulate *pharmaka*-consumption on the level of a whole population can be

found in the struggle against alcoholism in the 19th century. The so-called "gin-craze" of the 18th century was viewed as a massive societal problem.[3] Gin made alcohol consumption less expensive and more accessible, in particular for women. The 19th century then saw massive programs to combat the endemic alcohol-problem, in particular in the working-class. Modern equivalents can be seen in regulations such as the EU-regulation REACH (Registration, Evaluation, Authorization and Restriction of Chemicals) ((EG) No. 1907/2006).[4] The aim of this is to protect EU-citizens from intoxication by dangerous chemicals that can be found in all kinds of products.

On the level of digital *pharmaka* the General Data Protection Regulation (EU) 2016/679 (GDPR) looks like a first attempt to ensure something like the large-scale protection not just of individuals, but of a whole population. What Foucault described as "bio-politics", the attempts to direct the hygienic practices of a population, to prevent pandemics, to render the "body" of the people strong, has an *analogon* in political measures aiming at protecting and furthering the mental well-being of the population through systematic regulation of digital *pharmaka*: which would be the politics not of *bios*, but of *nous, noo*-politics.

e) Self enhancement — from caffeine to productivity apps
The importance of the rise of caffeine (and decline of alcohol) in Europe since the 17th century has been discussed at great length. New *pharmaka* can change societies for the better; the coffee-houses were not just spaces of open debate and intellectual exchange, but also provided a substance that would allow people to work and think more. The coffee-house in this sense also points to the necessity to frame new *pharmaka*, to control their use and to provide opportunities for the social exchange of experience with self-enhancement techniques. The equivalent of the coffee-house (or for that matter

---

3   Dillon, Patrick: The Much-Lamented Death of Madam Geneva. The Eighteenth-Century Gin Craze, London: Review 2002.
4   https://ec.europa.eu/environment/chemicals/reach/reach_en.htm (3.2.2022).

the tea-room) can be identified in the virtual spaces of the internet where people talk about their experiences with new self-enhancement technologies, for instance apps such as 'Headspace', or fasting apps.

However, coffee is not the only analogy that can be made. There are more severe substances of self-enhancement such as cocaine, low-dosage consumption of LSD, all kinds of "go-pills" or simply Ritalin. At this stage, we find it difficult to imagine a digital *pharmakon* boosting human performance so intensively that restrictions could become necessary.

f) Pandemic misuse — chemical and digital
The most commonly recognized example of mass misuse of a helpful substance is the pandemic consumption of sugar, causing millions of people to suffer from a fatty liver, diabetes or many other health problems. Cheap carbohydrates could also be classified as a substance almost equivalent to sugar, as they are easily convertes into sugar in the human body. Western societies are only just beginning to understand the pandemic scope of the problem. Fighting bad nutritional habits has been identified as a political challenge, since the health problems caused by overweight, diabetes and liver-failure are going through the roof. In the same way a pandemic of ADHD is calling the overuse of digital media into question, in particular among young children. As we have established that fighting bad nutritional habits is not a plausible individual challenge, but a societal problem, this insight should be used for the fight against the pandemic health problems caused by digital *pharmaka*. The most important lesson here seems to be that it will become inevitable to confront the economic interests of important and powerful players: multinational businesses which generate their profit by offering consumers the quick dopamine kick triggered by glucose, fructose, carbohydrates or digital communication.

g) Addiction, chemical and digital
The opioid-crisis in the US has shown what disastrous consequences an unskillful, profit-driven use of *pharmaka* can have. Opioids are of specific interest when it comes to the analogy of chemical and

digital pharmacology, because in this case the ontological quality (one might even say "essence") of the molecules has such evident impact on the way such substances are used or misused. Of course, opioids can be used in a skillful way as painkillers for short periods of time, as Stiegler also states. However, in this case, the addictive character and the massive impact on the human brain are so strong that strict regulation is needed.

Is there an equivalent of opioids in the digital sphere? It might seem a little exaggerated to think of online gambling as a highly addictive "substance", especially as there appears to be an important difference between chemical and digital *pharmaka* which is very relevant to the case of opioids: digital *pharmaka* can trigger the release of dopamine, certainly — but they cannot themselves replace it. At this point the analogy seems to have reached its limits. Whereas hard drugs such as opioids interfere immediately with the brain chemistry, digital *pharmaka* can only trigger the self-regulation of the messenger substances in the brain.

h) Employment protection
Nevertheless, we need to keep in mind that in both cases people do not expose themselves to chemical and digital *pharmaka* only by their own choice.

Most of the time, it seems that people allow chemical or digital *pharmaka* to enter their bodies because their jobs require it. In this sense a worker in a production plant exposed to chemical substances and a manager exposed to massive digital input could be viewed as analogous. In both cases the question of a collectively defined and legally permitted "maximum permissible dose" seems to be an appropriate response. Not to be forced to answer e-mails in the evening or on a weekend can thus be viewed as an element of employment protection, just as the protection from chemical exposure was defined from the late 19th century on. This, of course, is of particular importance for people working in call-centers or online services.

i) Class differences in self-medication
The analogy of chemical and digital "maximum permissible exposure" clearly raises the question of class differences. Champagne or beer, Cuban cigars or cheap cigarettes, the Italian opera or the brass band — naturally, class differences have always been important in the use of *pharmaka*. Today, there still seem to be important differences between underclass alcohol consumption and upper-class cocaine "self-medication". There are important differences between the consumption of beer (or for that matter gin) on the one hand, and cocaine on the other. Not only in sports do people attempt to distinguish themselves class-wise and to communicate class-identity (e.g. by playing tennis or lifting weights, as Bourdieu has shown): class distinctions and class-consciousness are also evident in the use of *pharmaka*.

They can now be conceptualized as tending towards self-programming and self-enhancement in the case of the upper-classes and distraction and confusion in the case of those exposed to poverty. Pharmacology as a project of emancipation would then hope to put everybody in a position which allows them to use *pharmaka* in a skillful and controlled manner. Just as reading was an important element in the emancipation of the working-class in the 19th century, we are now confronted with the challenge of achieving a new, digital alphabetization.

j) Protection of children
The analogy would also allow us to frame the protection of children from digital *pharmaka* in an appropriate way. Exposing small children to uncontrolled TV- or internet-consumption then can be viewed as a form of intoxication, i. e. mayhem. Criminal law would therefore have to be adapted to fit this new social condition. Again, collectively binding decisions are necessary to implement in the digital sphere what is common practice in chemical pharmacology. This would also force us to re-evaluate systematically the way children are exposed to digital *pharmaka* in schools. The class differences here are also evident: upper- and middle-class families protect their children by sending them to Steiner schools, while others see their chil-

dren constantly exposed to digital frameworks, even in elementary schools.

This would also imply the "protection of minors", the necessity of which is evident to everyone when it concerns alcohol, but which is by no means so widely recognized in the case of digital *pharmaka*: access to digital *pharmaka* needs to be restricted legislatively in the same way that other laws enforcing the protection of minors operate.

k) Restricted prescriptions/Regulations on who can prescribe what drugs to whom

The concept of digital pharmacology would also allow us to question who is allowed to prescribe what to whom. Once we reached an agreement that digital *pharmaka* should be treated like chemical *pharmaka*, it would become obvious that not everybody should be allowed to provide any and every kind of digital *pharmakon*. Every country has strict regulations on what substances can be prescribed by what kind of doctor, some regulations being more liberal and others more restrictive. Some kinds of digital *pharmaka*, in particular those developed as extensions of the gambling industry, should not be sold on an unregulated market. Just as pharmacies have the license to sell certain drugs, so digital businesses should be subject to selective or specialist legitimation of what they do and what they sell.

l) Military use of pharmaka

The use of poison gas by the German Reich in World War I was probably the first use of chemical substances for military reasons in modern times. The chemical industry soon became an important branch of the military complex. In World War II, the German military used what was called "tank chocolate": *Pervitin* was a substance which allowed German soldiers to fight in for three days without a break, as the German "Blitz" destroyed neutral Belgium.[5] Of course, Pervitin is just the most striking example of a military use of chemical *pharmaka*. Alcohol has, for centuries, fueled the aggression and

---

5   Ohler, Norman: Blitzed. Drugs in Nazi Germany, London: Pinguin 2016.

perseverance of soldiers. In the Vietnam war cannabis and heroin became important factors that influenced the state of the American Armed Forces. Today, suicide terrorists often intoxicate themselves with ketamine in order to overcome all inhibitions.[6]

In our modern age, evidently, digital *pharmaka* have become an element of warfare in our days. This is not only true for cyber-attacks which aim at infrastructures, but in particular for the "weapons of mass distraction"[7]: fake news, micro-targeting, (brain-)hacking, the influx of polarizing ideas and distracting topics in the news — all these elements are nothing other than the military use of digital *pharmaka*.

Up to now, all attempts to regulate or ban the use of these weapons seem to have failed. The only option left appears to be an equivalent of the gas mask, i.e. education, which may immunize citizens against the most destructive effects of digital *pharmaka* used as weapons. Framing the problem in this way will, hopefully, help people to understand the gigantic scope of the problem.

4.4 A community of learning citizens: towards a cura publica

Our presentation of the distinction between a liberal and a republican approach to digital pharmacology has helped, we hope, to show different options for dealing with the massive influx of digital *pharmaka* into our societies. The different elements have illustrated what a republican approach to the politics of digital pharmacology would look like: the pressure and complexity of dealing with new *pharmaka* would be seen as a common challenge, not as an individual task. The great strength of the analogy between pre-digital and digital *pharmaka* resides in the conclusion that it allows: no one would claim that dealing with complex pharmacological substances could

---

[6] See for example: Basra, Rajan: Drugs and Terrorism: The Overlaps in Europe, London: ICSR 2019, pp.24ff.; available at: https://www.icsr.info.

[7] The term was already used as the title of a television film in 1997.

plausibly be a private matter. Obviously, it is quite simply impossible for the individual to understand and use chemical substances alone, without external aid. No one would claim that finding out about appropriate medication should be the single individual's own responsibility. We need medical assistance, the expertise of psychiatrists and the regulation of the state in order to ensure use of pre-digital *pharmaka* in a skillful way. The same is true for digital *pharmaka*.

Digital *pharmaka* are *res publicae*, and therefore need to be dealt with in a collective effort, in a common, public and political framework. Only a *cura publica*, a common and public system of care will allow us to use digital *pharmaka* in a skillful way. Large-scale social-psychological health-care is not something human beings can provide on their own; it is not even something that should be left to families or civil society. In order to make sure that the *cura publica* is really public and political, we need to overcome a phase in which the influx of digital *pharmaka* is left to the private interests of the business sector.

In our view this new perspective has a variety of advantages in comparison to preceding attempts to react to the digital crisis. Drawing the conclusions we propose here from re-reading Rousseau will in our view help to overcome a paradigm that might be called "Kulturkritik", following the classical authors of the German Weimar Republic.[8] The digital crisis is not about "decadence" and not about *pharmaka* in general, but about finding and establishing new ways of applying them skillfully. Digital pharmacology is far from an attempt to ignore the great opportunities the new *pharmaka* offer. However, it puts the challenge in a larger perspective.

The German word "Sammlung" ("collection" as well as "contemplation") expresses the idea of a both material and intellectual effort to counteract entropy: As in Richard Long's Circle of Stones, which is reprinted on the cover, collection allows contemplation — and

---

8   Examples would be authors such as Oswald Spengler, Ernst Jünger, Carl Schmitt, Hans Frayer. In a wider sense, Adorno's essays could be viewed as "Kulturkritik" as well.

vice versa. We view Richard Long as an artist of neg-entropia, of "Sammlung".

Part II: An Interview with Bernard Stiegler

Bernard Stiegler: Elements of Pharmacology
An interview with Felix Heidenreich and
Florian Weber-Stein[1]

Concept, analogy, metaphor, art

Q: We would like to start by talking about the concept of *pharmakon* and pharmacology. In our view it is a key-concept in your body of thought, a kind of center of gravity of your philosophical work. It is a very complex term. How did you come across this term? When did you start to use it?

Stiegler: Oh yes, the term is indeed crucial. I developed this concept at the beginning of the year 2000, when I was the head of IRCAM, the "Institut de Recherche et Coordination Acoustique/Musique" at the Centre Pompidou in Paris. Back then, we were trying to understand contemporary music, and I sought to develop the theory of what I call "general organology". We attempted to consider instruments and scores as "organs", but also extended this view to devices like radio-sets or more sophisticated hi-fi-sets. At the time, we needed a common conceptual ground which would allow us to understand music and musical practice in an interdisciplinary setting. Then I enlarged the concept of general organology so as to be able to apply it to everything — not only music, but really *everything*. Every human activity. And this concept of general organology was a kind of methodology for organizing interdis-

---

1 Stuttgart and Paris, 26th June 2020

ciplinary and transdisciplinary cooperation among representatives of different spheres of thought, for example biologists, anthropologists, historians, philosophers, economists, engineers. The idea was, and still is, that you have three levels of organs: a) biological or "endosomatic" or psychosomatic organs, b) artificial organs — let's call those tools and instruments, technologies — and c) social organizations. We tried to understand how these levels interact. The proposition was to provide a methodology for evaluating the level of toxicity of technology in a specific context. For example, you know that technology for water can be very good in the context of an industrial society, but it can also destroy an economy in India. So, the idea behind "general organology" was to understand how the three levels of organs interact, what the ramifications of specific ways of using organs are. In many cases the long-term effects of new organs can only be understood in hindsight.

So this was the point of departure of the concept. Then I realized that the terms *"pharmakon"* and "pharmacology" might express more clearly what was on my mind. Of course, I was a student of Jacques Derrida and so I used the concept of *pharmakon* in the context of Socrates and his critical writings — but it was not my point of departure. Even though I find, of course, Derrida's text on Plato binding and extremely necessary and very useful and in fact not only useful but magnificent — I nevertheless do not consider it at all sufficient.

Q.: It is impossible to sum up Derrida's text "Plato's Pharmacy" since it is also partly a collage of citations which does not intend to have *one* point or to express *one* argument.[2] However, the text shows a movement in which we understand that the spoken word (*la parole*) is not the perfect, pure or transparent position which allows us to overcome the complexity, ambiguity, and difficulty of writing (*l'écriture*). Plato seems to suggest that writing is ambiguous, dangerous, misleading, toxic. Only the spoken word in a dialogue is capable of really expressing adequately what needs to be said, Plato seems to

---

2   Derrida, Jacques: "La pharmacie de Platon", in: Jacques Derrida (Ed.), La dissémination, Paris: Seuil 1972, pp. 77–213.

be saying. Derrida, however, shows us that we can never completely leave the cave. We can move from one cave to another, from *écriture* to *parole*, but there is no getting outside the cave, "pas de hors-texte". We wonder if you would agree with this way of describing Derrida's reading of Plato. It also seemed very important to us that Derrida mainly refers to the *Phaidros*, whereas you focus on the *Protagoras*. Why do we end up with a different picture when we take into account the *Protagoras*?

Stiegler: The *Protagoras* shows more clearly the ambivalence, the two-faced character of all *pharmaka*, Prometheus and Epimetheus, intoxication and remedy, danger and help. Derrida was absolutely right to show that Plato was wrong when he thought that with dialectics it was possible to overcome the limitations created by writing. Derrida argued that the general circumstances of writing set the conditions for *critical* writing, so there will never be a really critical form of writing, capable of criticizing from the outside. And there is a systematic problem: with Derrida you don't have any positive discourse on the *pharmakon*. It is a philosophy of deficiency, if you like: there is no positive side to the *pharmakon* for Derrida, and this is a problem for me, because in my view the decisive question is how to transform a poison into a remedy. This is a question for everything, for all kind of artifacts. An artifact is necessarily something that disturbs an equilibrium. The writings of Rousseau reflect such a disturbance, and Socrates' critique of rhetoric could also be viewed as a way of responding to a disturbance of an established equilibrium by the introduction of a new technology or *pharmakon*. However, such a perturbation can be good and even necessary if it is the occasion for producing a leap in individuation, as Gilbert Simondon tried to show in his writings about individuation.[3]

Q: So in your view, Derrida's thinking remains "aporetic" in a specific sense. Derrida himself wrote a text on the *aporia*, which literally means the place where you cannot cross the river, where there is

---

3   Simondon, Gilbert, L'individuation à la lumière des notions de forme et d'information, Grenoble: Millon 2005.

no *poré*, no ford, no passage.⁴ Derrida's thinking always seems to aim to get deeper into the aporia, not to overcome it: the aporia of hospitality, the aporia of friendship and politics, the aporia in our relation to animals.

Reading your work and your dialogues with Derrida we had the impression that you agreed with Derrida's view on metaphysics. You seem to concur with Derrida that "writing" is not something purely exterior, not just a tool we can use or not use. It is a *pharmakon* which enters our bodies, transform our brains. However, you seem to say that there are different ways of "using" the *pharmakon* — and that philosophy has something to say about these ways. The term "using" is maybe inappropriate, because it still seems to presuppose the distinction between inside and outside...

Stiegler: Well in my view, the decisive distinction is between *adoption* and *adaptation*. You might also call it the skillful and the unskillful use, if you like. If you are experienced, you can practice an adoption, you can use morphine as a painkiller, if necessary, for a short period of time, at the correct application rate. However, if you are inexperienced and you just adapt, you might end up as an addict. In our society — in every society — *pharmaka* are necessary, unavoidable. However, to say that *pharmaka* are absolutely necessary is not the same as to be naïve about this necessity. This necessity can be also a very bad necessity in the sense of *anagké* for the Greeks. *Anagké* is the Greek term for fate, the tragic fate. So to deal with the tragedy of this situation we need to instantiate what I call a general organology — the goal of which is to address the conditions of possibility for a positive pharmacology.

Q.: Would you agree that the term or the idea of the *pharmakon* is also put forward in opposition to this idea of the tool, which does not really change me? — I use a tool, I can drop it, but it does not enter my being, whereas the *pharmakon* from the start — and of course scripture and writing are the paradigms — changes me, transforms

---

4   Derrida, Jacques: Apories. Mourir, s'attendre aux "limites de la verité", Paris: Galilée 1996.

me. It is not like a knife that I can drop; and even if I view the knife as a *pharmakon* I would then see that the knife changes the person that holds it: through having the knife they are a different person than the person they would have been without it. So we would ask if this is an important point in your view. What would be the counter-concept of *pharmakon*?

Stiegler: Well, the term "tool" refers to an object, whereas the term *"pharmakon"* refers to a relationship. In my terminology, therefore, everything can be a *pharmakon*. Everything. Your wife, husband or partner can be a *pharmakon*. Even a theory can be a *pharmakon*. If for example, you are Marxist and you use the theory of Marx in order to navigate through the world, it becomes a *pharmakon*. And this *pharmakon* can become toxic, if it becomes an ideology. In this case you change your relationship to the words, although the theory stays the same.

Q.: We were wondering to what degree *pharmakon* is a metaphor and in what sense it is a concept. We concluded that maybe it is both. It is an analogy, but it also has a literal sense: The claim seems to be that *pharmaka* actually enter, impact and even transform our brains. To say that music is *like* heroin is not just a metaphor, it is also *literally* true: a teenager using heroin and a teenager practicing music will have transformed brains in both cases, impacted differently, of course, but still in both cases we will see the neurophysiological impact. In both cases the *pharmakon* is not exterior to the body, but in the body, in the brain. What is your view on this question? Is pharmacology actually a discipline of reflecting, training, "practicing" our relationships?

Stiegler: Absolutely. Pharmacology is not a theoretical enterprise. Of course, there is theory in pharmacology, but only as it serves the practice of pharmacology. Pharmacology is practical knowledge, a *prâxis* in the way Aristotle described ethics and politics. How do we "practice", for example, the hammer? The hammer is, as you know, an important example for philosophers, for Heidegger and Wittgenstein and many others. The hammer can be simply another tool, just a device, but it can also be the instrument of a specific culture. And in such a case, the hammer transforms the body and mind of a true craftsman. This is maybe not the case for an unskilled laborer, but it is true for someone who has spent years working with a hammer in order to create specific stones, e.g. a mason. For him the hammer is not a tool, but a *pharmakon*: he feels the hammer in his hand and cannot help being transformed. His tools are his friends, he has known them for many years, knows how they react, how they can help him.

I first realized this when I was trying to understand what happens in the relationship between musicians and their instruments. Arturo Benedetti Michelangeli — the very famous pianist — was particularly known for interpreting Claude Debussy. He is maybe the most important performer of Debussy, since his magnificent interpretations have shown a new Debussy. One day he came to Paris to perform at the Salle Pleyel and I listened to him on the radio. It was a live program. It was a very, very important event in Paris in 1979. He had announced that he would be playing "La cathédrale engloutie" by Claude Debussy, which is extremely difficult to play, a long and very complex piece of music. And he entered the stage at the Salle Pleyel, which was at this time the most important concert hall in Paris. He sat down in front of the piano and he stayed silent, and he just didn't play. One minute went by, then two minutes, on the radio. Then he suddenly said: "My piano is cold." And he stood up and he left the place. It was a scandal, an absolute scandal. All the journalists said that he was just a diva. But I thought: not at all! The piano is a part of himself. And even if it is separate in terms of outward appearances, it's not really separated internally from his own being. And I understood what he meant when he said the piano was cold.

So I think I understood that the relation to objects is essential. It is the case with everything. If you are creating a good relation to a thing, an object, it is in a sense an object of addiction. Donald Winnicott puts emphasis on this at the beginning of his work on the transitional object in "Playing and Reality" (1971); he says on the first page that the teddy bear for the small child is addictive. And the problem is: it's a good addiction, it is a necessary addiction and the 'good enough mother' will be able to tell the time at which it is necessary to consider it a bad addiction and to leave the teddy bear behind. So here the mother practices pharmacology for the child. For me Donald Winnicott is a very important thinker because he shows that the *pharmakon* is a source of the beginning of the construction of the personality and the maturing psychological apparatus. The human mind evolves through the relation to *pharmaka*.[5]

No ontology of *pharmaka*, but savoir-faire

Q: You are employing the concept of pharmacology in such a broad concept that one could almost say that the human condition is pharmacological, not *homo sapiens*, not *homo ludens*, but *homo pharmacans*. You highlighted the fact that the concept is so attractive to you because *pharmaka* can be interpreted as a poison and a cure. So can you say a little bit more about the criteria for differentiating between positive and negative aspects of the *pharmaka* we use? Or is that something which is only possible for us to see in hindsight? Can we differentiate between *pharmaka* that are bad *per se* and *pharmaka* which leave more room for development and adoption instead of adaptation?

Stiegler: No *pharmakon* is bad *per se*. Even the atomic bomb, for example. Why? Because the toxicity and the creativity depend on the situation. That is the accidental character of the situation. This is what is tragic about the human situation: There is always this conflict between Prometheus and Zeus: using too much or too little, at the wrong moment, in the wrong dose. But this is a projection of something that is irreducible in human life. As you know, the god of pharmacy, Asclepius, has two serpents. Snakes are a very common symbol for the ambivalence of a *pharmakon*, because it is at the same time a poison and the remedy. And for thousands of years it

---

5   This recourse to Winnicott is outlined in B. Stiegler: What Makes Life Worth Living.

has been extremely important to cope with the ambivalence of the snake. This is why you find snakes as symbols everywhere, in China, in Japan, in Siberia, actually everywhere in Africa, in South America, in North America.

So the history of mankind is a constant struggle to practice adoption and to avoid adaptation, to "use" *pharmaka* without abusing them. The two snakes are there from the start.

Q: If a snake can be positive or negative, if even an atomic bomb can be helpful (although we might be hard put to think of such a situation) — then does this mean there is no ontological quality of a specific *pharmakon* at all? The toxicity of substances to us seems very different, and in some cases this toxicity shows itself when we look at large-scale use of different *pharmaka*. If we compare for example the mass use of *khat* in Somalia today and the use of chamber music in Austria in the 19th century, the long term-consequences seem very different. And these consequences seem to be defined not only by the way these two *pharmaka* are used, but also by the ontological character of the two *pharmaka* themselves. This may be an extreme and, in a way, a false example, but for us an important question is: aren't there at least different classes of substances that we can distinguish, even if we don't judge their character normatively or morally? Take, for instance, the case of caffeine and heroin? Both can be misused, but still there seems to be something in the substance itself, doesn't there?

Stiegler: Well, the effects of these substances can depend on the circumstances. I do in fact think that an ontology of *pharmaka* is not possible. This is why Heidegger is still important.

Q: Heidegger who claimed: "The essence of technology is nothing technological." Heidegger thought that modern "technology" was a way of looking at the world, a specific "understanding of Being". So, this could mean that it is not in the things, but in our relationship to the things. For us, speaking from a German background, it is very important to see that in France Heidegger's philosophy of technology is considered important. It is a pity we cannot enter into the details of your philosophical debate with Heidegger outlined in "Technics and Time, 1: The Fault of Epimetheus". Heidegger's personal pharmacology was rather strict. He had no TV, and would spend months in his cabin in the Black Forest. And there are his remarks on the "world of motorways". The motorway to him seemed to have metaphysical meaning; it was a symbol of what he called the "planetarian movement". Somehow it seems to be difficult not to categorize some *pharmaka* in this way.

Stiegler: I really think that there's no ontology for *pharmaka*. However, there are criteria for evaluating or understanding pharmacological effects. There are, I think, two possible criteria. The first one is knowledge. This may sound simple, but it is not that simple. When you are capable of transforming a poison into a remedy, it is because you have developed a knowledge of this *pharmakon*. And you can tell yourself or other people, "Don't use it, it's very dangerous". This is what many experts do, doctors, or, for example if you are a mathematician you can critically assess the use of geometry in architecture. You can predict what is possible and what isn't, and in order to define the limits of what can be built you can use your skills as an expert. In this first sense, there is something similar to science necessary.

Q: The term "skill" is being used in a certain sense here, right?

Stiegler: Well, a "skill" means that something can be reproduced, trained. It is in a way technical knowledge. The emphasis on skills in modern education should therefore be questioned. OK, some skills are necessary, but there is more. The second criterion is different. I would like to call it "savoir" in French, because "knowledge" in English sounds as if it was just referring to academic knowledge, to a knowing-that. However, for me pharmacology is not at all about academic or scientific knowledge only, but also about everyday life knowledge, about experience, about knowing-how. This is most obvious in sports, for example, or cooking. Or the upbringing of children is also a "savoir-faire". The French term *savoir* covers these two elements.

Q.: "Savoir-vivre" is also about taste, isn't it?

Stiegler: Absolutely. Taste needs to be formed by experience. This is why aesthetic education is so important for our children. Now for me all kinds of knowledge or *savoir* are "negenthropic". That would be a more scientific way of putting it: toxicity is entropy, *savoir* produces negentropy. Heroin-addiction destroys the brain's capacity to produce its own substances and consequently the brain relies on the input of heroin. The brain then is less complicated: it has, if I can put it this way, more entropy. However, if you manage to use *pharmaka* in order to build up complexity, you produce negentropy.

Q.: This is also a very important point in your work: there are entropy and negentropy, dispersion and collection. Digital pharmacy can distract us terribly. However, it is interesting to see that in the history of European culture there is a long tradition of distraction. Some of Mozart's greatest pieces are called *divertimento*. Culture is also very much about distraction, about fighting contemplation in theaters, in opera houses, in the cinema...

Stiegler: Distraction is not *per se* a problem. You are right to claim that many aspects of European culture are *pharmaka* that offer distraction, *divertimento*, and so on. However, distraction becomes problematic when it turns into a large-scale production of what is called "Je-m'en-fous-tisme" ("I-don't-give-a-fuckism") in French: a poisoning neglect, indifference, moral insensibility, the pandemic absence of taking-care.

Q.: That is a mechanism that you described in "Taking Care of Youth and the Generations" as a gigantic machine operating in order to confuse and distract people. We will come back to this topic later. This "art" of using the right *pharmaka* in the right way is what defines the history of mankind. But can we tell what is use and what is abuse? The difference between *adaption* and *adoption* on the one hand seems plausible intuitively; on the other hand, these two modes seem intertwined, often hard to distinguish.

Stiegler: Well, it is an extremely tricky art or craftmanship. In some cases, it is hard to tell. Even heroin was used by artists such as Charlie Parker, John Coltrane or Jimi Hendrix. I don't think that bebop would have been possible without heroin. So even such a dangerous *pharmakon* can be used in order to serve a purpose. And then of course, we have an endless number of examples of the skillful use of *pharmaka*, from the Hopi in New Mexico (who were so important to Aby Warburg) to all sorts of ways of using music, dance, chemicals, tea, coffee, theory, theology — whatever. Anything can be helpful or harmful. In French we call such a situation "casuistique". This term refers to the Jesuit tradition of solving difficult legal or theological questions in a case-by-case approach. There may be some heuristics, but there is no general framework that will deliver ready-made answers.

Q: This almost sounds like an Aristotelean idea of *phronesis* or *prudentia*, practical wisdom.

Stiegler: Well, the difference is that Aristotle could presuppose a well-ordered *kosmos* full of teleology, full of natural, given *teloi*. For him, an ontology of *pharmaka* was still possible. He tried to *find* the right answers, whereas we have to *invent* them.

The subject of pharmacology: auto-therapy

Q.: In this framework there would also be no "point zero", no absolute soberness. Human beings are always in a relation to the world, so there is always an "already", a *toujours déjà*, in pharmacology. Even soberness could become a *pharmakon*. Of course, you know the entire tradition of deconstructing the idea of the Ego and the Cogito and the idea of the sovereign subject in French post war philosophy. There is no "pure" or "sober" Cogito. There is a philosophical question implied here: how should we think the subject of pharmacology?

Stiegler: Well, of course I would agree that autonomy is not possible, but it is possible to take care of oneself, which is, in a way, analogous to an adoption of one's heteronomy. "Taking care" is important to me, *cura*. What I called "savoir" could also be viewed as a therapy. Nietzsche already had this therapeutic vision of philosophy. Of course, we also have to view this philosophy as a *pharmakon*. Derrida's style of deconstruction has become for some people a *pharmakon* by which they are almost intoxicated, which is tragic. They repeat Derrida's style although Derrida himself never repeated anything. Georges Canguilhem in his writings about thought and thinking turning into an ideology has some wonderful descriptions of this tipping-point. Such knowledge not only can, but always will become a *pharmakon* itself. So, in order to answer your question: we don't have to imagine the subject to be a sovereign *cogito* in order to understand that it can have an auto-therapeutic relation to itself; it can practice what Foucault called the care for the self.

Q: I think this is a very important point: that in a way what used to be autonomy in the European tradition — or the idea of the autonomous subject, particularly in the liberal tradition — then becomes "autopharmacology." Autopharmacology is not the same as autonomy, since we are never the complete masters of our *pharmaka*. Would that be a way of putting it?

Stiegler: I completely agree. And I do think that it is extremely important to get these things right. You see, when Derrida was young and published his first books, deconstruction was something very theoretical. Today in France, the contestation of autonomy is a daily experience. Today, everybody knows that there is no sovereign subject. So, the questions of autonomy and heteronomy are posed in a different context. If you adopt a therapeutic point of view, you always operate with the assumption of a quasi-causality. You will never be able to prove what really helps; you have to believe in your empowerment. And you have to try to make good health possible, although you know that in the end you will fail. You cannot "produce" good health, and eventually you will die anyway, but good health is always a possibility.

Q: However, we wondered if you would agree that maybe there's something like a class difference in regard to pharmacology. Different social classes not only differ in their income and wealth, but also in regard to what Bourdieu called "cultural capital". A decisive part of this cultural capital is the competence in using *pharmaka* in a skillful way. What people inherit (or do not inherit) is the skill of pharmacology. Could we re-describe class-stratification in terms of pharmacology? Bourdieu would argue that cultural capital is distributed unequally, and that there are systematic reasons why the children of the internet-managers in Palo Alto are put into Steiner-schools, and protected from digital intoxication.

Stiegler: Oh yes, of course there is a correlation between pharmacological skills and social class. Digital *pharmaka* are poured into society and the skills are distributed very unequally. Some people have to work in call-centers, others don't. There is an analogy to other toxic substances. A higher social status allows you to avoid contact with dangerous chemicals, at least in some cases. Rich people have their personal assistant to do all the e-mailing for them. And of course, there are very unequal options for protecting your children from digital *pharmaka*. However, the correlation is not absolutely clear. It is like in the case of alcoholism, which can be found across the board, in all social contexts. Indeed, the introduction of gin and the following "gin craze" in England had a harder, almost epidemic impact on the lower classes. In particular women were introduced to alcoholism in a new way. Gerald Moore wrote brilliantly about this disruptive change in drinking behavior in England in the 19th century. The impact of gin was incredible. However, gin also affected the upper classes. Evidently, there is also upper-class alcoholism — and there are also rich people who are addicted to their smartphones. I have many friends who are from the French bourgeoisie and even high-bourgeoisie, and they have problems to keeping their fingers from their smartphones. In my view, the class difference is not even so important. I think what has been happening in the last 20 years is a disruptive influx of new *pharmaka* — and in this case there is not so much competence you can inherit.

New *pharmaka* disturb things, and I am not sure that the old class structures can simply absorb such a rapid influx.

The writing self and the digital self

Q.: This is an extremely important point for the idea of digital pharmacology: You claim that we are witnessing the introduction of new *pharmaka* — and that this process can be understood in analogy to historical examples. Could you tell us more about the way you conceptualize the emergence of a digital pharmacology in contrast to a pre-digital pharmacology?

Stiegler: Well, I think we can learn a lot from earlier examples of new *pharmaka* being introduced into a society. The radio is not just a medium that will help you to transmit messages, but when it started to become an element of mass-culture, it changed our hearts and minds. In the 1950s and 60s rock'n roll was a new, a mood-transforming *pharmakon*. And already back then the older generation was appalled by the "yeah-yeah"-music (that was the term back then in France). It's usually the younger generation that absorbs new *pharmaka* right away. So as a mother or a father, you are in a way always too late. Today it is often our children who teach us digital pharmacology. Our non-digital experience may probably help us, but it is not clear in what way exactly. There are other possible comparisons that might help us to understand what is going on more properly.

Q: Maybe we could look at ourselves in analogy to the indigenous people in North America when they were confronted with alcohol. We are not experienced with these new digital *pharmaka* that are coming from California and China (in most cases), and like the First Nations we now have to learn as fast as possible. You seem to be sceptical about the option of using our older experiences with other *pharmaka*. On the other hand, you suggest that we might counter the dangerous new *pharmaka* with something that we know better, older *pharmaka*. In your case this would be the defense of the practice of reading and writing, which in Europe has a long tradition.

Stiegler: Oh yes, of course reading and writing are absolutely essential in Europe. It was very important for me to see in what way the Chinese culture of reading and writing differs from the European. The experience in China made me understand the relevance of Foucault's work on reading and writing more clearly. There is this wonderful text by Michel Foucault about "Writing the Self" (1983).[6] It is a tiny, magnificent text, written only a short time before he died. In Foucault's work on the "techniques of the self" writing and reading play an essential role. It is very important to see that Foucault shows that Seneca's teachings are not about mere erudition, but that they intend to transmit wisdom, the wisdom of using reading in writing in order to take care of ourselves. The way we think, feel, what we are — all this is linked to the *pharmakon* of reading and writing. Foucault described it beautifully, although he didn't use Derrida's term *pharmakon*. Foucault uses the term "governmentality". It is a pity and even a bit ridiculous that Foucault and Derrida just could not discuss things with one another, although there would have been so much to talk about. Modern research shows that Foucault was right. I'm thinking in particular of the book by Maryanne Wolf.[7]

Q: In her book *Proust and the Squid* she shows in what way reading forms and transforms the human brain. She compares the brains of persons who read the Latin alphabet, the Chinese script and the Japanese mixed Kanji writing system, and the two-syllable-alphabets. Her research seems to suggest that these three groups of readers actually have almost different brains. So, when Foucault talks about the fact that a discourse "inscribes" itself in the subject ("s'inscrit") we can now see that this is not just a metaphor. The brain actually changes: there is a true neuro-plasticity. You also call this process a process of "grammatization"...

Stiegler: Yes, I do think that philosophy absolutely needs to take this research into account. Reading is an education of your attention-

---

6 M. Foucault, Michel: "L'écriture de soi".
7 M. Wolf: Proust and the Squid, 2008.

spam, of the way you perceive the world. We should, however, remember that reading used to be considered dangerous and toxic. Up to the 20th century, in many families, parents would tell their children not to get lost in books, not to read so passionately, not to be addicted to books. And then there were of course institutions like the church which tried to control what could be read and what couldn't. The priest would tell you how to use the *pharmakon* of reading and what not to read. It is very important to understand that the Bible can be seen as a dangerous, even toxic *pharmakon*. There is a text by a Portuguese Jesuit priest saying explicitly that the most powerful substance that was brought to America was the Bible. The term "grammatization" refers to a form of constructing or creating subjects on the basis of reading and writing.

Q.: In Germany, there are several books which propose a "bibliotherapy". For every difficult situation in life they recommend a specific novel. Books are "prescribed" in order to self-medicate your moods.[8] There is even an Italian editing house, Mondadori, with an advertisement saying: *Un libro per ogni emozioni* — a book for every emotion. To view the Bible as a *pharmakon* would also continue the line of thought of Foucault. You explicitly refer to Foucault, but you propose talking about "psycho-power" instead of "bio-power". Foucault talked about the way institutions such as the military or schools form our bodies, and produce a memory of the flesh. In contrast, you emphasize the absence of discipline in contemporary psycho-power: power by distraction and confusion, not by discipline. We were wondering to what degree this perspective addresses a general tendency.

Stiegler: Foucault's analysis of bio-power is very important to me. His reconstruction of disciplinary power, and even his description of neoliberalism, however, describe a society which is not the one we

---

8   Berthoud, Ella/Elderkin, Susan, with Bünger, Traudl: The Novel Cure. An A to Z of Literary Remedies, Edinburgh: Canongate Books 2013.; Schönberger, Margit/Bittel, Karl Heinz: Die literarische Notapotheke: 100 Romane für alle Lebenslagen, München: Knaur, 2014.

live in today. In his perspective, power is all about the optimization of production: schools, universities, the job market, self-marketing — all of this tries to create a subject which is willing and able to produce to the maximum. In "From Bio-power to Psycho-power" I tried to show that we live in a different society. Today we live in a society which tries to maximize consumption; psycho-power produces not primarily discipline, but confusion, carelessness. Foucault cannot help us, I'm afraid, to understand in what way psycho-power tries to cut the links between generations. Our cultural heritage is attacked because it prevents us from enjoying maximized consumption.

Q.: Your defense of the European tradition of reading and writing the self could be pushed one step further: we are currently completely losing the tradition of "learning by heart". The generation of our grandparents knew dozens, if not hundreds, of poems by heart. Is that another *pharmakon* we might rediscover? Could that be an antidote to digital dementia? Or would that just be a case of regressive nostalgia?

Stiegler: To have several *pharmaka* at your disposal is definitely an advantage. Not to mention older *pharmaka*, and not losing our knowledge about them, which in my view is essential. This is not a reactionary or conservative point of view. I do not claim that older *pharmaka* are *per se* better than new ones. The ethics of taking care is neither left nor right.

Q.: We would like to go back to the historical comparisons. You said that the influx of new *pharmaka* can disrubwhole societies. We have briefly touched on the topic of the introduction of writing in ancient Greece, the introduction of gin in England, the introduction of beat music in France. You claim that once again we are seeing the turbulences created by a new *pharmakon*. Your latest book is entitled *The Age of Disruption*.

Stiegler: I think that this is exactly what we are witnessing at the moment, and have been experiencing for the last 15 years. We are all overwhelmed by the sheer quantity of digital *pharmaka*. This is why the whole planet is intoxicated: men and women, animals, plants, everything. We really have to be absolutely clear about this. We are going through a crisis of mass-intoxication. I am working with poor families in the North of Paris, working-class families, where absolutely everyone is intoxicated with smartphones: the parents, the children, even the babies. The brains of our children are under attack, and this attack is occurring at a mind-boggling pace.

Q.: At the same time older *pharmaka* seem to be losing importance. It is striking to see that "violence" (which could also be viewed as a *pharmakon*) is, at least in most of Europe, not normal anymore. It is very interesting to see that a "bar brawl" or "pub fight" was considered to be an element of normal Sunday afternoon behavior for many centuries, both in Europe and in North America: On Sunday, after holy mass, men would drink and fight at the local pub. This custom was even recognized in penal law and the punishment was very mild, if it existed at all. Beating up or even raping your wife was normal, and even the public torturing of criminals was a common spectacle. Clearly, we are still witnessing much too much violence, maybe even the rise of new forms of violence, but we also seem to be letting go of some of the very harmful older *pharmaka*, don't we? Schivelbusch[9] describes in his cultural history of drugs that for many centuries people in Europe were more or less constantly drunk. So maybe the decline in alcohol consumption, and in the practice of violence and religion have created an opening for the new *pharmaka*? Does this explain the rise of new, digital *pharmaka*, this demand for the replacement of classics like religion, violence and alcohol?

Stiegler: It is always the case that newer *pharmaka* replace older ones. Whether it is a step forward or a step backwards has to be decided on a case-by-case basis. It seems to me, for example, that today's generation of young adults who grew up with social networks are less absorbed by telecommunications technology than their (infantilized) parents. They seem to crave for social relationships, for

---

9   W. Schivelbusch: Tastes of Paradise.

which — unfortunately — most social media are often only a poor substitute. However, I am skeptical as to whether a downward trend can really be determined in the level of violence. Rather, it seems to me that violence is taking on ever more subtle forms.

Q.: We would also very much like to hear more from you about the combination of different *pharmaka*. In German there is a specific term for mixing multiple drugs: "mixed consumption" ("Mischkonsum") means, for instance, that people use heroin *and* cocaine, they use caffeine to get up in the morning and alcohol to get to sleep at night. Of course, this is maybe more an empirical than a philosophical question, but to us it seemed very important to see that the digital intoxication you talk about often goes hand-in-hand with specific kinds of chemical mass-intoxication. We are thinking not only of the gigantic consumption of sugar, caffeine and alcohol in Western societies, but also of drugs like aspirine, ibuprofene, paracetamol, Prozac, Ritaline, Valium, cannabis etc. The reciprocal effects seem to make digital pharmacology extremely difficult. Gaming and cannabis-consumption often go hand-in-hand, and maté-based soft drinks were popular in the hacker-scene long before they entered student-life. However, we seem to know very little about the way all these *pharmaka* interact. Maybe digital *pharmaka* push people towards anti-depressants, but maybe it is the other way around. As a society we seem rather lost. You already mentioned that you consider the American "war on drugs" to be a disaster. Do you place any hope in the new "techniques of the self" that are gaining importance: Yoga, Meditation, MBSR?

Stiegler: With my partners and friends, and in my collaborative networks, we are working very hard and exactly to gain and distribute new pharmacological knowledge and competence. Of course, digital tools can also be used as a remedy. What makes all of this so difficult is the incredible pace involved. This influx is happening a lot faster than the earlier historical examples you mentioned. This is why, it seems to me, our societies have become destabilized.

Q.: However, it seems to be the case that digital *pharmaka* are not only being mixed with other (analogue) *pharmaka* — with the possible effects of mutual reinforcement or moderation. The same applies to digital *pharmaka* vis-à-vis other digital *pharmaka*. Think for example of different apps on the very same smartphone. Some apps (e.g. Amazon or eBay) want to seduce me into consuming (ever more), others provide me with music, but at the same time present data on my moods, depending on the time of day (e.g. Spotify) etc., while yet others act as an antidote to absorption in consumption: they remind me of my daily meditation exercise, they advise me to go to bed earlier, they help me to identify harmful ingredients in cosmetics, and so on. Does this plurality make something like *consumer sovereignty* possible?

Stiegler: The term "consumer sovereignty" is ill-chosen, because sovereignty is in itself an illusion. I prefer to call this the adoption of one's inevitable heteronomy, and this of course remains a possibility in the digital era. There are choices left to us: It is hard, but not impossible to navigate in the Internet without relying on Google's hegemonic search engine; we don't have to take advantage of Facebook's "single sign-on"-service, etc. We still have at least some discretionary space to decide for ourselves which drugs we want to be affected by and can try to find antidotes to the poisons. What is more, there are genuine examples of new forms of sociality that are made possible by networking media. One might think here of local platforms that help organize neighborly assistance and for instance offer our help (for shopping and other errands of everyday life) to older people in times of corona.

Q: So a lot of things are similar. But still there is something decisively new about digital pharmacology. On the one hand it is just another kind of *pharmakon*, but on the other hand there is something new going on. Could you help us to disentangle this riddle?

Stiegler: The first difference is speed. The influx of alcohol in America took centuries, but now everything is happening incredibly fast. You have to imagine what "digitalization" means, not only in Europe, but in Latin America, Africa etc. Within a few years our world has completely changed. Millions of smartphones have been produced, as well as tablets and other gadgets. And this process seems to be accelerating. A new technology or app can be outdated within months. Human beings have to have time in order to understand new *pharmaka*, but no sooner have we partly understood one kind of addictive app than there is already the next on the market: Facebook, Twitter, Instagram, TikTok, it never ends. So in my view the speed of influx is an important factor, since it makes it a lot more difficult to practice adoption. Speed pushes us towards adaptation. Adoption takes time.

The second difference is the degree of automation,[10] which has increased immensely. Nowadays not only our practical knowledge, our *savoir-faire*, is being made superfluous by the mechanization of production, as in Fordism; even our theoretical skills and our capacity to form a will and make decisions are "aided" by so called "artificial intelligence" (which is, in fact, artificial stupidity).

Q.: A concrete example would be helpful in understanding this. Are you referring here to the mechanism of "parsing", which means that every human input into an algorithm has to be "translated" into another format so that it can be processed further? — Facebook, to give only one prominent example, has "solved" the problem of parsing by short-circuiting the input-giver. Whenever you begin to type in a word in order to characterize yourself, your text is then completed by a pre-given list of possible answers. You cannot escape the virtual logic of the drop-down menu. Thus the design of the human-machine interface determines the data entry process, so that the user cannot but fulfill the task of assigning their details to a semantic category registered on the server side.[11]

---

10   On this see Stiegler, Bernard: Automatic Society, Volume I. The Future of Work, Cambridge et al.: Polity 2016.
11   This example is taken from Mühlhoff, Rainer: "Big Data Is Watching You. Digitale Entmündigung am Beispiel von Facebook und Google", in: Rainer Mühlhoff/Anja Breljak/Jan Slaby (Eds.), Affekt Macht Netz. Auf dem Weg

Stiegler: This is a very illuminating example of the way in which digital technologies intervene in our perceptions of opportunities, and hence influence our decision-making processes. Selections are taken over by prefabricated options that are tailored through "user profiling" and "auto-completion" technologies. This form of assistance can be of great help, of course. Think of "Google Translate", for example, which I use a lot, because I cannot speak Chinese. It enables me to communicate with people I could otherwise not address; but to the effect that the nuances of speech are flattened out and that my message is depersonalized. A third difference comes into play here. There is a theory tacitly inherent in the use of computers and smartphones: the idea that everything can be solved by calculation. And this, of course, is absolutely wrong. Nothing can be solved by calculation. You always need a decision that is not calculable. Derrida has written about this at great length: the really important things like hospitality, love, forgiveness, politics, etc., have a blind spot. If you can explain your love by calculation, it is not love.

Q.: This was almost a *leitmotif* in his later writings. Only an "impossible", i.e. incalculable, unlegitimizable friendship is friendship. In this sense a "Facebook-friend", to Derrida, is not a friend. Friends never exist in the form of a given, but only as a possibility that can be addressed in the vocative. In this regard Montaigne's phrase "Oh my friends, there are no friends!" suddenly makes sense...

Stiegler: Indeed, Facebook epitomizes an industrialization of friendship on an unprecedented scale. It is made possible by the digital grammatization of our social relationships, which reconfigures these by virtue of algorithmic calculations. The "making" of friends on Facebook is largely "out-sourced" to a technical function through which everyone in my address book automatically gets an invitation to become my friend. I would argue that as a result of this kind of automation, our social relationships are at risk of being proletarianized, i.e. mentally impoverished, and that the real exchange of ideas,

---

zu einer Sozialtheorie der Digitalen Gesellschaft, Bielefeld: transcript 2019, pp. 81–107.

recognition and disclosure, which Aristotle linked with friendship, or *philia*, is prevented.[12] And since friendship is the basis of larger social entities called community, I would go so far as to claim that the so called "social networks" can be very harmful to our social connections.

The underlying process can be coined "digital grammatization", i.e. the process of analyzing and formalizing human behavior into a code that can be digitally processed. For example, the Facebook user is stripped of his personality, he is disindividuated, by being broken down by the algorithm into a series of data which he — in part on a voluntary basis, but to a growing extent involuntarily — discloses by navigating through the Facebook sites, by liking and disliking and showing his interest/disinterest etc. It is on the basis of these data that social networks form connections, make suggestions and thus determine the rules of our communalization, or transindividuation, as I prefer to out it with recourse to Simondon.

Q.: That sounds as if you were assuming a technological determinism according to which social organization is determined by the technical organs. But isn't digital grammatization also pharmacological in the sense you explained above? In your book "Taking Care of Youth and the Generations" you convincingly show the pharmacological character of the leap in (pre-digital) grammatization that occurred as a result of the invention of the printing press, followed by the Reformation, the Counter-Reformation and finally the Enlightenment (whose passionate striving toward registration and categorization is beautifully exemplified by Diderot's project of the *Encyclopédie*). All these events brought about not only an increased normalization and standardization (of language use and behavior as a whole), which made the individual the subject of state control, but also created the public sphere as a "critical space".[13] Do you also see positive aspects associated with the digital grammatization

---

12 For a deeper elaboration on this see Stiegler, Bernard: "Five Hundred Million Friends: The Pharmacology of Friendship", in: UMBR(a): Technology 17 (2012), pp. 59–75.

13 See B. Stiegler: Taking Care of Youth and the Generations, p. 138ff.

brought about by social media platforms? Can we use the existing tools for social networking in a non-proletarianizing or subversive way, based on "algorithmic literacy", i.e. a critical knowledge of the mechanisms that are at work? Or do we need alternative digital technologies — hardware or software — in order to counter the anti-social effect of current "social media"?

Stiegler: Of course, I do see the chance for a renewal of social life on the basis of the unprecedented formalization of social relations due to digital grammatization, and the social networks could well add to this development. The enthusiasm of young people for social networks is an indication of the longing for social relationships in an anomic world, and I am convinced that something good can be created from this. There is no denying the fact that Facebook is a largely a marketing tool which has newly defined the terms for personalized targeting. However, Facebook does not necessarily corrupt its users. For example, the self-profiling demanded by Facebook can strengthen your reflective powers, instigating a practice of auto-ethnography which might generate a heightened awareness of the conditions and the importance of social bonding. Knowledge of what you are doing (and of what is done to you) when you navigate on Facebook is absolutely important. We need to arrive at an understanding of these networks both on the social and technological level. I don't like the term "algorithmic literacy", because it sounds like standardized knowledge, like a prefabricated competence. But you are right that a minimum level of understanding of the technical mechanisms underlying social networking is helpful.

Q.: So again, it is not technology *per se* that is dangerous...

Stiegler: Well, we have to see that the ideology of calculation and the digital *pharmaka* go hand-in-hand with a neoliberal mindset. I say this explicitly, because it is extremely important to understand that Silicon Valley is the last stage of what I call ultra-liberalism. The rise of neoliberalism goes back a long time. When it entered the political stage with Thatcher and Reagan in the 1980s, all the theory was there already, in particular Hayek. And Hayek said: everything is calculable. Gary S. Becker even applied the model of the *homo oeconomicus* to the mother-and-child-relationship.[14] This was the reason for him to think that neoliberalism was better than any other kind of political economy. And this is the reason why he said we don't need any government, we don't need any state, we need only to the market decide everything. Silicon Valley is based on such a kind of libertarianism and the most developed discourse on that is transhumanism. As you know, the transhumanists intend to replace mankind by machines which are stronger than any human being.

Q: Do you think this is a real danger? From a continental European point of view it sounds just like science-fiction-madness…

Stiegler: What is dangerous is the mindset. You can address a medical question, for instance, only through judgment, i.e. the diagnosis by a doctor or a collective of doctors. You need a "faculty of judgement", an "Urteilskraft" in Kant's terminology, not just calculation. The corona-crisis could not have been anticipated based on data from the past. It takes more than just calculation to make intelligent decisions…

Q.: Would it be appropriate to use Kant's distinction between *reasonable* ("*vernünftig*", *Vernunft*) and *rational* ("*verständig*", *Verstand*) in order to describe what is missing in pure calculation?

Stiegler: That is indeed a very valuable distinction, but one which is nowadays almost forgotten. In the wake of the Industrial Revolution, the spiritual, or *noëtic* dimension of intellectual life was almost absorbed by the ratio, or the computational faculty of the mind. Reason is for Kant, first and foremost, the faculty of envisaging ends, or what I prefer to call critical protentions. Reason is entrusted with the question of what goals are valuable, and how I can achieve those goals without preventing others from pursuing theirs — in short: how I ought to live. In a society determined

---

14   Becker, Gary S.: A Treatise on the Family, Cambridge, MA: Harvard University Press, 1981, Enlarged ed., 1991.

by consumption, these questions no longer arise; the satisfaction of needs is short-circuited by the permanent presentation of objects that seem desirable through marketing. This is why Adorno and Horkheimer called consumer capitalism a new form of "barbarism" — and rightly so. However, with the advent of computational capitalism, things have gone even further. Operations of understanding, which are now mimicked and taken over by machines and algorithms, are exosomatized and thus in a literal sense split off from the synthetic functions of reason. This amounts to a state that I call generalized madness, which means that an immense process of disinhibition takes place. And this is characteristic of contemporary capitalist societies.[15]

Q.: The connection you draw between the rise of capitalism and the process of disinhibition is not yet completely clear to us. In his groundbreaking work on the "civilizing process" Norbert Elias seems to claim quite the opposite: that modernity is characterized by the development of inhibition, or affect control, which he characterizes as the "dampening of spontaneous flashes (and) restraint of affects"[16]. Affect control is traced back by Elias to the sociogenetic process of social differentiation, which begins with the emergence of the territorial state and the abolition of feudal structures, but is then further promoted by the development of capitalism. From a completely different angle, Foucault also seems to suggest a connection between the disciplining of society, which is evident in the criminalization of deviance and supported by institutions like school and prison, and the development of modernity, of which capitalism is an important aspect. Against this backdrop, could you specify what you mean by "disinhibition"?

Stiegler: I do not find anthropological conceptions particularly helpful that distinguish, in a scholastic vein, between ratio and affect.

---

15   On this see B. Stiegler: The Age of Disruption.
16   Elias, Norbert: The Civilizing Process, Volume.I. The History of Manners, Oxford: Blackwell, 1969; Elias, Norbert: The Civilizing Process, Volume II. State Formation and Civilization, Oxford: Blackwell, 1982.

Such dichotomies are too abstract, and fail to grasp the interconnectedness between the three levels of organs which I outlined at the beginning of our interview. I prefer the term *libido*, inherited from psychoanalysis, or the conception of libidinal economy, by which I understand the way in which we take (or do not take) care of objects. In principle, two tendencies of libidinal economy can be distinguished, one based on short circuits, dominated by mere drives which aim to consume their object; and the other, based on long-circuits, brought about by a sublimation of drives which opens up room for attention, the formation of will and finally results in care for their objects.[17] Against this background it can been seen that the systematic short-circuiting of our libido by psychopower, which I call disinhibition, leads to a corruption of the will and splits off the analytic functions of understanding from reason, or a practice of care. Disinhibition in this sense does not mean that actions will be guided by mere "affect", that is, will be devoid of any calculation or instrumental rationality — quite the contrary: Jean-Baptiste Fressoz aptly refers to modernity as a process of "reflexive disinhibition".[18]

A school of pharmacology

Q.: One possible starting point to change the prevailing mindset would be the school system. Foucault was fundamentally skeptical about school because he sees it primarily as a "disciplining dispositive". Although he never made an explicit analysis of educational institutions, in the course of his historical reconstruction of the emergence of modern institutions like hospital and prison, school as well is in the focus of attention as one modern institution through which the conditions, attitudes, and behaviors of its subjects are formed. These have less to do with the content of teaching than with the type

---

17 This theory is outlined in B. Stiegler: What Makes Life Worth Living, p. 24f.
18 Fressoz, Jean-Baptiste: L'apocalypse joyeuse. Une histoire du risque technologique, Paris: Le Seuil 2012, p. 160.

or the form of teaching. You seem to be more optimistic that school may have an educating function in the humanist sense.

Stiegler: Foucault is right to stress that school is about training, or rather, instilling discipline, although this is just one effect. A further point is that school takes care of the "transindividuation of knowledge", an important part of which is the passing on of knowledge from one generation to the next. It constitutes in itself, through this very function, a system of care.

Q.: In the aftermath of the PISA-study, beginning in the year 2000 the European school systems started to undero a change, from "input-orientation" to "output-orientation". The curriculum is no longer defined by the knowledge to be imparted, but rather by skills that the students are intended to acquire. What do you think about this paradigm-change?

Stiegler: I think that knowledge is extremely important. But, in a way, we have to re-invent what knowledge is. Because today we are not producing knowledge. As you said, we are producing skills. We are producing competence. But for me knowledge is not at all skill and competence. Knowledge is the capacity to produce singularity in a singular situation, i.e. to produce a purely single answer. A skill is not at all singular. It is always standardized. And this is the effect of industrialization, and now we have to enter into a new form of industry: let's call it the industry of post-intoxication. Children have to learn how to overcome the stage of intoxication, "intoxication" being understood here, of course, not only as that of alcoholics and other drug addicts. So there is a new political economy being erected on the basis of this intoxication.

Q: You do not only reflect theoretically about questions regarding the design of the educational system. You were a member of the "Agence nationale de la recherche" for a while. In 2008 you were asked by Vincent Peillon, at the time Minister of Education in France, to lead a group on the introduction of digital technology into school. What were your plans? And why did you eventually resign?

Stiegler: In 2008 the approach was wrong. It was dominated by Microsoft and the general understanding of the computer as a "computing machine". However, I am still working on establishing an alternative digital culture. In the suburbs north of Paris[19] we are using two big tools or programs, softwares and databases. The first one is an information-modeling technology for the building and construction sector. It is completely transforming urban development, urban programming, planning etc., thereby making a new structure possible for cities. And we use this video game called Minecraft, albeit as a free software version ("Minetest"). I am now launching a campaign in France to completely change the character of national education. For me, national education should become a laboratory at all levels: from kindergarten to high schools and universities the understanding of a computer must be changed completely.

Q.: One seems to find traces of a positive digital pharmacology here…

Stiegler: The Internet has great potential, the most remarkable of which is that it breaks up the opposition between consumption and production. The problem is not the internet itself, but its embeddedness within computational capitalism. However, there are collaborative technologies, and a kind of a struggle for free software, a growing community subscribing to the principle of "open source" and "creative commons" — these are practices which are not covered by the logic of algorithmic governmentality, and which foreshadow a *practice of care*.

---

19   For more information on the Stiegler project "Pleine Commune", see PROJET D'EXPÉRIMENTATION TERRITORIALE PLAINE COMMUNE TERRITOIRE APPRENANT CONTRIBUTIF (http://francestrategie1727.fr/wp-content/uploads/2016/02/projet-plaine-commune-10.03-bernard-stiegler.pdf).

Q: You described pharmacology as a "savoir-faire". It's a kind of art or craft; on the one hand it is an individual, a self-educational project, if you like — you have to know what is good for you in a way. The stoicism Foucault worked on was in a way an individualistic movement. On the other hand, pharmacology is a political challenge. It's also something that we have to decide on together. Even if prohibition wasn't very successful and even if the war on drugs is a disaster — still it is something we somehow do together. We don't know if you would agree with this difference between, if you like, a liberal or even neoliberal pharmacology, and what may sound almost like a French Republican idea of democratic *collective* self-determination.

Stiegler: Well, I agree that digital pharmacology is not a realistic individual project. However, I am not sure that the national level is the right level and that the French Republic is a good model for implementing helpful collective decisions. In my experience there are other helpful models that operate more on the basic level of community work. In our work in the north of Paris we are trying to learn from the experience of people like Gregory Bateson. We use the concept of the Alcoholics Anonymous as they were studied by him. Bateson showed very clearly that if an alcoholic wants to stop drinking, the best way is to help another alcoholic to stop drinking. The bad experience, the tragic experience of alcoholism is the destruction of self-esteem. But this experience can give you the competence which allows you to help others. Suddenly you transform the experience into knowledge from which you can benefit. The efficiency of this association is four times better than the efficiency today, for example, of hospitals. I recall this example, because I consider the question of new forms of knowledge to be something which has to play out on the level of localities. I don't believe in top-down pharmacology, but in people helping themselves. So, I think here the question is to re-invent and re-establish a proper idea of "knowledge". Intelligent machines can make their users more stupid and we have to cope with the fact that we are producing a new proletariat.

Q: This is a very important observation for which there is even some support from a few empirical studies on France. One could hope that machines would do the stupid work for us, and that humans would do the intelligent work, coding machines etc., but this seems not to be the case. In fact, very few people actually code and a lot of people are told by algorithms where to deliver the parcels. Richard Sennett has worked a lot on the decline of craftsmanship. In this regard it seems that by your account digital pharmacology is almost a game-changer. It is so toxic that the positive use of digital tools depends on the re-inventing of the computer, you claim. And you outlined the political circumstances under which re-invention and re-contextualizing might be possible, but this seems to have almost utopian character. What makes you think that in the end we will really survive the onslaught of digital *pharmaka*?

Stiegler: Failure is simply not an option. We have already talked about *pharmaka* as soft power. The United States and China are dominating the production of digital *pharmaka*. If we don't manage to answer this challenge, European companies might disappear. Even Mercedes or Volkswagen can disappear. Everything can be destroyed by China and America, if we don't manage to defend a European way of life. I think that this European singularity can be described as a culture of hyper-retention: a culture of books, both in the Greek and in the Jewish tradition. This culture of textuality is different from the Chinese tradition of writing. I hope and believe that we can preserve this. The reason for which I believe that it is possible is because it is reasonable. The way in which Silicon Valley is developing everything is rational, but completely unreasonable. And this produced Donald Trump. And it is not only me who says so. They are saying that today in Silicon Valley itself. So in order to establish and develop a European digital pharmacology we should stop emulating American or Chinese models. We therefore have to re-evaluate locality, and this is a question of what I call a new political economy.

Q.: In this example too, as in the case of the Bible, the term *pharmakon* also seems to describe a weapon. You can not only intoxicate yourself, but also others. And if we are understanding you correctly, you're saying that organizing our *pharmaka* together is also a way of keeping our weapons polished, as it were, and ourselves prepared for self-defense. *Pharmak*on as a weapon; there is this term: "weapons of mass-distraction".

Stiegler: Oh yes, of course. America's strength in the 20th century was not at all the GIs. The GIs lost in Vietnam. The strength of America was Mickey Mouse, Hollywood and art. But you see, the wounds we have can also be a starting point of a healing. This is an old romantic idea, of course, but you can also imagine it in a more practical sense. Django Reinhardt, the French gypsy musician, lost two fingers, and after the accident he became the famous musician that we will never forget. Before this traumatic event he was already an excellent musician, but after the accident he became a genius. I think it is extremely important to understand that the accidents, the toxicities, the diseases, our wounds, can also be sources of invention, creativity, maybe even of the most brilliant ideas. So, from all the intoxication, all the misuse of *pharmaka*, we may also learn – and progress and practice pharmacology together.

Bibliography

Works by Bernard Stiegler

Stiegler, Bernard: Technics and Time, vol 1: The Fault of Epimetheus, Transl. Richard Beardsworth and George Collins, Stanford: Stanford University Press 1998.
Stiegler, Bernard: »The Discrete Image«, in: Derrida, Jacques/ Stiegler, Bernard (Eds.), Echographies of television. Filmed Interviews, Cambridge: Polity Press 2002, pp. 145–163.
Stiegler, Bernard: Taking Care of Youth and the Generations, Transl. Stephen Barker, Stanford, CA: Stanford University Press 2010a.
Stiegler, Bernard: »The Carnival of the New Screen: From Hegemony to Isonomy«, in: Pelle Snickars/Patrick Vonderau (Eds.), The YouTube reader, Stockholm: National Library of Sweden 2010b, pp. 40–59.
Stiegler, Bernard: »Pharmacology of Desire: Drive-based capitalism and libidinal dis-economy«, in: New Formations 72 (2011), pp. 150–161.
Stiegler, Bernard: »Five Hundred Million Friends: The Pharmacology of Friendship«, in: UMBR(a): Technology 17 (2012), pp. 59–75.
Stiegler, Bernard: »Die Aufklärung in the Age of Philosophical Engineering«, Computational Culture 2 (2012b), http://computationalculture.net/die-aufklarung-in-the-age-of-philosophical-engineering/ (01.02.2021).
Stiegler, Bernard: What Makes Life Worth Living. On Pharmacology, Cambridge et al.: Polity Press 2013.
Stiegler, Bernard: »The Most Precious Good in the Era of Social Technologies«, in: Geert Lovink/Miriam Rasch (Eds.), Unlike Us

Reader. Social Media Monopolies and their Alternatives, Amsterdam: Institute of Network Cultures 2013, pp. 16–30.
Stiegler, Bernard: »Licht und Schatten im digitalen Zeitalter«, in: Ramón Reichert (Ed.), Big Data. Analysen zum digitalen Wandel von Wissen, Macht, Ökonomie, Bielefeld: transcript 2014, pp. 35–46.
Stiegler, Bernard: Automatic Society, Volume I. The Future of Work, Cambridge et al.: Polity Press 2016.
Stiegler, Bernard: The Age of Disruption. Technology and Madness in Computational Capitalism, Cambridge et al: Polity Press 2019.
Stiegler, Bernard: »Elements for a General Organology«, in: Derrida Today 13 (2020), pp. 72–94, DOI: 10.3366/drt.2020.0220.

Other cited works

Abbinnett, Ross: The Thought of Bernard Stiegler. Capitalism, Technology and the Politics of Spirit, London: Routledge 2017.
Arendt, Hannah: On Revolution (orig. 1963), London: Faber & Faber 2016.
Basra, Rajan: Drugs and Terrorism: The Overlaps in Europe, London: ICSR 2019.
Becker, Gary S.: A Treatise on the Family, Cambridge, MA: Harvard University Press, 1981, Enlarged ed., 1991.
Benkler, Yochai: The Wealth of Networks. How Social Production Transforms Markets and Freedom, New Haven/London: Yale UP 2007.
Berthoud, Ella/Elderkin, Susan, with Bünger, Traudl: The Novel Cure. An A to Z of Literary Remedies, Edinburgh: Canongate Books 2013.
Bloch, Marc: Feudal Society, 2 Volumes, Chicago: The University of Chicago Press 1961.
Bösel, Bernd: »Der psychotechnologische Komplex — Die Automatisierung mentaler Prozesse als demokratietheoretisches Problem«, in: Zeitschrift für Politikwissenschaft (2021), https://doi.org/10.1007/s41358-021-00283-2.

Bottici, Chiara: »Democracy and the spectacle: On Rousseau's homeopathic strategy«, in: Philosophy and Social Criticism 41 (2015), pp. 235–248.
Castells, Manuel: The Rise of the Network Society. The Information Age: Economy, Society, and Culture. Volume I (orig. 1996), New York: John Wiley & Sons, 2nd edition, 2011.
Cinnamon, Jonathan: »Social Injustice in Surveillance Capitalism«, in: Surveillance & Society 15 (2017), pp. 609–625.
de Baecque, Antoine : Le corps de l'histoire. Métaphores et politique (1770–1800), Paris : Calmann-Lévy 1993.
Dent, Nicholas J.H./O'Hagan, Timothy: »Rousseau on Amour propre«, in: Proceedings of the Aristotelian Society 72 (1998), pp. 57–75.
Dent, Nicholas J.H.: Rousseau. An Introduction to his Psychological, Social and Political Theory, Oxford: Blackwell Publishers 1988.
Derrida, Jacques: »La pharmacie de Platon«, in: Jacques Derrida (Ed.), La dissémination, Paris: Seuil 1972, pp. 77–213.
Derrida, Jacques: Apories. Mourir, s'attendre aux "limites de la verité", Paris: Galilée 1996.
Derrida, Jacques: De la Grammatologie. Paris: Editions de Minuit 1967.
Diamond, Larry: »The Road to Digital Unfreedom: The Threat of Postmodern Totalitarianism«, in: Journal of Democracy 30 (2019), pp. 20–24.
Diderot, Denis: »De la poésie dramatique«, in: Denis Diderot (Ed.), Œuvres esthétiques Paris: Garnier 1959, pp. 179-287.
Dillon, Patrick: The Much-Lamented Death of Madam Geneva. The Eighteenth-Century Gin Craze, London: Review 2002.
Elias, Norbert: The Civilizing Process, Volume I. The History of Manners, Oxford: Blackwell 1969.
Elias, Norbert: The Civilizing Process, Volume II. State Formation and Civilization, Oxford: Blackwell 1982.
Foucault, Michel: »L'écriture de soi«, in: Dits et écrits, Paris: Gallimard (Quarto) 2001, t. II, n° 329.
Foucault, Michel: The History of Sexuality, Volume I: An Introduction, New York: Pantheon 1978.

Fressoz, Jean-Baptiste: L'apocalypse jouyeuse. Une histoire du risque technologique, Paris: Le Seuil 2012.

Gullstam, Maria: Rousseau's Idea of Theatre. From Criticism to Practice, Doctoral Thesis in Theatre Studies at Stockholm University, Sweden 2020, http://www.diva-portal.org/smash/get/diva2:1430104/FULLTEXT01.pdf (20.11.2021).

Gutman, Huck: »Rousseau's confessions: A Technology of the self«, in: Michel Foucault/Luther H. Martin/Huck Gutman/Patrick H. Hutton (Eds.), Technologies of the Self. A Seminar with Michel Foucault, Amherst: University of Massachusetts Press 1988, pp. 99–120.

Haas, Michaela: "Wir bekommen Twitter Gehirne", NZZ-online, 27.3.2019 https://www.nzz.ch/folio/wir-bekommen-twitter-gehirne-ld.1622968 (10.9.2021).

Harari, Yuval Noah: »Why Technology Favors Tyranny«, in: The Atlantic (2018), https://www.theatlantic.com/magazine/archive/2018/10/yuval-noah-harari-technology-tyranny/568330/ (01.02.2022).

Hayles, N. Katherine: »Hyper and Deep Attention: The Generational Divide in Cognitive Modes«, in: Profession (2007), pp. 187–199.

Hayles, N. Katherine: How We Think. Digital Media and Contemporary Technogenesis, Chicago, IL: University of Chicago Press 2012.

Hobbes, Thomas: De cive, ed. Howard Warrender, Oxford: Clarendon Press 1983.

Hunt, Lynn: Inventing Human Rights. A History, New York (NY)/London: Norton 2007.

Kohn, Margaret: »Homo spectator. Public space in the age of the spectacle«, in: Philosophy & Social Criticism 34 (2008), pp. 467–486.

Kolesch, Doris: Theater der Emotionen. Ästhetik und Politik zur Zeit Ludwigs XIV, Frankfurt a.M./New York (NY): Campus 2006.

Lakoff, George: »Metaphor and War: The Metaphor System Used to Justify War in the Gulf«, in: Martin Pütz (Ed.), Thirty Years of Linguistic Evolution. Studies in honour of René Dirven on the occasion of his 60th birthday, Philadelphia/Amsterdam: John Benjamins 1992, pp. 463–482.

Lakoff, George: Metaphor and War, Again. UC Berkeley 2003, https://escholarship.org/uc/item/32b962zb (01.02.2022).

Moore, Gerald: »The pharmacology of addiction«, in: Parrhesia 29 (2018), pp. 190–211.

Mosher, Dave: »High Wired: Does Addictive Internet Use Restructure the Brain?«, in: Scientific American (2011), https://www.scientificamerican.com/article/does-addictive-internet-use-restructure-brain/ (01.02.2022).

Mühlhoff, Rainer: »Big Data Is Watching You. Digitale Entmündigung am Beispiel von Facebook und Google«, in: Rainer Mühlhoff/Anja Breljak/Jan Slaby (Eds.), Affekt Macht Netz. Auf dem Weg zu einer Sozialtheorie der Digitalen Gesellschaft, Bielefeld: transcript 2019, pp. 81-107.

Münkler, Herfried: »Arzt und Steuermann: Metaphern des Politikers«, in: Herfried Münkler (Ed.), Politische Bilder, Politik der Metaphern, Frankfurt a.M.: Fischer 1994, pp. 125–140.

Musolff, Andreas: »Political metaphor and bodies politic«, in: Urszula Okulska/Piotr Cap (Eds.), Perspectives in Politics and Discourse, Amsterdam: John Benjamins 2010, pp. 23–42.

Nathan, Usha Manaithunai: On the Possibility of Visual Literacy and New Intentions with Digital Images, National University of Singapore 2011, https://core.ac.uk/download/pdf/48646006.pdf (01.02.2022).

Neuhouser, Frederick: »Rousseau und die Idee einer 'pathologischen' Gesellschaft«, in: Politische Vierteljahresschrift 53 (2012), pp. 628–645.

Neuhouser, Frederick: Rousseau's Theodicy of Self-Love. Evil, Rationality, and the Drive for Recognition, New York: Oxford UP 2008.

Ohler, Norman: Blitzed. Drugs in Nazi Germany, London: Penguin 2016.

Ozouf, Mona : »Régénération«, in : François Furet/Mona Ozouf (Eds.), Dictionnaire critique de la Révolution française, Paris : Flammarion 1988, pp. 821–831.

Ozouf, Mona: L'homme régénéré. Essai sur la Révolution française, Paris : Gallimard 1989.
Przepiorka, Aneta/Małgorzata, Blachnio/Miziak, Agata/Czuczwar, Barbara/Jerzy, Stanisław: »Clinical approaches to treatment of Internet addiction«, in: Pharmacological Reports 66 (2014), pp. 187–191. https://doi.org/10.1016/j.pharep.2013.10.001.
Reckwitz, Andreas : Das hybride Subjekt. Eine Theorie der Subjektkulturen von der bürgerlichen Moderne zur Postmoderne, Weilerswist : Velbrück Wissenschaft 2006.
Rheingold, Howard: The Virtual Community Homesteading on the Electronic Frontier, Reading: Addison-Wesley Publishing Company 1993.
Roberts, Ben : »Rousseau, Stiegler and the aporia of origin«, in: Forum for Modern Language Studies 42 (2006). pp. 382–394.
Ross, Daniel: »Pharmacology and Critique after Deconstruction«, in: Christina Howells/Gerald Moore (Eds.), Stiegler and Technics, Edinburgh: Edinburgh University Press 2013, pp. 243–258.
Rousseau, Jean-Jacques: Collection complète des œuvres de Jean-Jacques Rousseau, 17 volumes, Genève 1780–1789.
Schivelbusch, Wolfgang: Tastes of Paradise. A Social History of Spices, Stimulants, and Intoxicants, New York: Vintage Books 1993.
Schönberger, Margit/Bittel, Karl Heinz: Die literarische Notapotheke: 100 Romane für alle Lebenslagen, München: Knaur 2014.
Sewell, William H.: A Rhetoric of Bourgeois Revolution. The Abbé Sieyes and What is the Third Estate?, Durham: Duke University Press 1994.
Shapiro, Andrew: The Control Revolution. How the Internet Is Putting Individuals in Charge and Changing the World We Know, New York: Public Affairs 2000.
Simondon, Gilbert: L'individuation à la lumière des notions de forme et d'information, Grenoble: Millon 2005.
Sontag, Susan: Illness as Metaphor, New York: Vintage Books 1978.
Sontag, Susan: On Photography, New York: Delta Books 1977.
Spaemann, Robert: Reflexion und Spontanität. Studien über Fénelon, Stuttgart: Klett-Cotta 1990.

Starobinski, Jean: »The Antidote in the Poison: The Thought of Jean-Jacques Rousseau«, in: Jean Starobinski (Ed.), Blessings in Disguise; or, The Morality of Evil, Transl. Arthur Goldhammer, Cambridge: Harvard UP 1993, pp. 118–168.

Tinnell, John: »Grammatization: Bernard Stiegler's Theory of Writing and Technology«, in: Computers and Composition 37 (2015), pp. 132–146.

Tufekci, Zeynep: »How social media took us from Tahrir Square to Donald Trump«, in: MIT Technology Review (2018), https://www.technologyreview.com/2018/08/14/240325/how-social-media-took-us-from-tahrir-square-to-donald-trump/ (01.02.2022).

Wolf, Maryanne: Proust and the Squid. The Story and Science of the Reading Brain, New York: Harper Perennial 2008.

Wolf, Maryanne: Reader, Come Home. The Reading Brain in a Digital World, New York/London/Toronto/Sydney: Harper 2019.

Zuboff, Soshana: Surveillance Capitalism. The Fight for a Human Future at the New Frontier of Power, London: Profile Books 2019.